Designing Sensible Surveys

Ministry of Education, Ontario
Information Centre, 13th Floor,
Mowat Block, Queen's Park,
Toronto, Ont.   M7A 1L2

Designing Sensible Surveys

Donald C. Orlich
Professor of Education and Science Instruction
Washington State University
Pullman, Washington

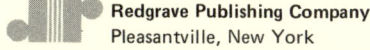 **Redgrave Publishing Company**
Pleasantville, New York

Copyright © 1978 by Docent Corporation, Pleasantville, New York

All rights reserved. No portion of this book may be reproduced by any process or technique, without the formal consent of the publisher.

Please direct all inquiries and orders to the publisher.

> Redgrave Publishing Company
> A division of Docent Corporation
> 430 Manville Road
> Pleasantville, New York 10570

Printed in the United States of America.

TABLE OF CONTENTS

	PAGE
PREFACE	iii
CONTENTS	v
LIST OF TABLES	viii
LIST OF FIGURES AND MODELS	iv

CHAPTERS

    1. USING A SURVEY TO COLLECT DATA 1

        Focus 2

        USING PRINTED INSTRUMENTS 3

        The Questionnaire: Advantages and Disadvantages 3

        General advantages 4

        Disadvantages of a questionnaire 7

        TWO OTHER INFORMATION-COLLECTING TECHNIQUES 8

        The Interview: Advantages and Disadvantages 8

        Interview types 9

        Conducting an interview 10

        Disadvantages 11

        Telephone Interviews 12

        The Interview Schedule 13

        ADDITIONAL GUIDELINES TO DETERMINE SURVEY USE 15

        Sample Survey Budget 16

        Wages 16

        Services 16

        Materials 16

        Training Costs 17

		PAGE
CHAPTERS		
2.	DESIGNING THE ITEMS	19
	PLANNING FOR ITEM CONSTRUCTION	19
	Parsimony	20
	Specificity	21
	Respondents' Knowledge	24
	Interest	25
	Single Variable Items	26
	Simplicity	28
	Sensitive Areas	29
	Semantics of Construction	32
	Manageability	36
	Avoiding Bias	37
	Positive Wording	39
	ITEM SEQUENCING	40
	Logical Leads	40
	Question Placement	41
	In Sum	42
3.	DESIGNING RESPONSE MODES	43
	MODES OF RESPONSE	43
	Forced-response Categories	43
	Exhaustive and mutually exclusive	44
	Categories for multiple responses	44
	Open-ended questions	45

CHAPTERS	PAGE
Convenience of form	48
ESTABLISHING APPROPRIATE SCALES	49
Nominal Scales	49
Ordinal Scales	50
Likert scales	52
Interval Scales	56
Transforming Items	57
Other Considerations	59
4. CODING SURVEY ITEMS	62
FORCED-RESPONSE CODES	62
Coding nominal data	62
Coding ordinal and interval items	63
Coding Likert scale items	64
Coding subscales of Likert scale items	65
OPEN-RESPONSE CODES	69
Coding open-ended items	69
Coding checklist items	70
ELECTRONIC DATA PROCESSING	73
Coding	74
Precoding	76
Column assignments	76
Row codes	78
Subdividing into groups	81

CHAPTERS		PAGE
5.	CONDUCTING THE SURVEY	84
	SAMPLING CONSIDERATIONS	84
	Random Techniques	85
	Drawing	86
	Using random numbers	86
	Stratified Samples	86
	Systematic Techniques	88
	Sample Size	88
	Disproportional Sampling	89
	COMMUNICATING WITH THE TARGET POPULATION	91
	Written Correspondence	91
	Follow-ups	92
	Is the Nonrespondent a Factor?	99
	PROTECTION OF HUMAN SUBJECTS	100
	INCLUSIONARY LANGUAGE	103
	Other Examples	104
	ONE PLANNING TECHNIQUE	105
6.	ADAPTING OTHER DESIGNS	108
	OTHER EFFECTIVE METHODS	108
	Delphi Technique	108
	One Example	111
	Advantages of the Delphi	112
	Disadvantages of the Delphi	112
	Adapting Statements of Intended Policy	116
	Needs Surveys	119

CHAPTERS		PAGE
	An example for in-service needs	120
	Couplet Designs	126
	ONE MORE WORD	130
7.	ANALYZING THE DATA	132
	DESCRIPTIVE TECHNIQUES	132
	Respondent Counting	132
	Percentages	136
	Means	139
	INFERENTIAL STATISTICAL TESTS	144
	Use of Two Statistical Tests	145
	Chi Square	145
	Rank Order Coefficient of Correlation	147
	BROADER IMPLICATIONS OF ANALYSIS	149
	Generate testable hypotheses	149
	Compare results with other disciplines	150
	Mandate subgroup analyses	150
	Challenge the sample	151
	Attendant impact	151
8.	WRITING THE RESEARCH REPORT	153
	PLANNING THE REPORT	153
	Writing Style	154
	Do not use trite phrases	154
	Minimize personal references	154
	Be careful of Latinized singular and plural forms	154

CHAPTERS	PAGE
Select the precise term	154
Using "significant difference"	155
Format	155
Abbreviations	155
Tense	156
Source citation	156
Avoiding prejudicial terms	157
PARTS OF THE RESEARCH REPORT	158
Introduction	158
Methods	158
Respondent Population	158
Survey instrument	158
Procedure	159
Results	159
Discussion	161
Appendix	162
General	162
In Conclusion	163
APPENDIX	164
REFERENCES	187
INDEX	191

List of Tables

TABLE		PAGE
4-1.	Scoring of Reversed Questions	66
4-2.	Two Alternative Coding Systems	67
4-3.	Representative Data Response Models	80
5-1.	Estimated Population and Sample Sizes	89
5-2.	Hypothetical Population	90
5-3.	Percentage of Returns and Follow-up Techniques	96
5-4.	Questionnaire Response Waves and Follow-up Techniques	97
6-1.	Ten Selected Final Responses from the State of Washington Delphi Survey to Determine Goals for Common Schools	113
7-1.	Relationship of Age and Sex of Respondents	134
7-2.	Data Display Concerning Distribution and Return of Questionnaire	137
7-3.	Simulated Number of Different Daily Preparations of Home Economics Teachers	138
7-4.	Tabulation of Question Three (Simulated)	139
7-5.	Code to Convert Scaled Items to Means	140
7-6.	Preliminary Calculations for Mean or Ratio Scores of Likert Items	140
7-7.	Tabulation of Ranked Items (Simulated)	142
7-8.	Calculation of Mean Preference for Administration (Simulated)	143
7-9.	Responses in Contingency Table Format	147
7-10.	Model of Rank Ordered Items	148
8-1.	Example of Frequency Distribution Table (Simulated)	159

List of Figures and Models

FIGURE OR MODEL		PAGE
1-1.	One Type of Interview Schedule	14
3-1.	A Sample of Likert Responses	55
4-1.	Combining Checklist and Likert Designs	72
4-2.	Typical Electronic Data Processing Card	75
4-3.	Subdivision of Two Questionnaire Items for Subgroup Analyses and Comparisons	81
5-1.	Suggested Postcard Follow-up	92
5-2.	Sample Cover Letter	93
5-3.	PERT Network for "Typical" Survey Project	106
6-1.	Partial Science Survey	118
6-2.	Abstracted Administrator Needs Assessment Instrument	122
6-3.	Abstracted Teacher Needs Assessment Instrument	124
6-4.	Selected Illustration of Modified Couplet Design for Surveys	128
8-1.	Example of Bar Diagram	160
A-1.	Basic Questionnaire Format	166
A-2.	Modification of Response System	173
A-3.	Key Punch Modification	175
A-4.	Adaptation of Coding System	177
A-5.	Optical Scan Instrument	179
A-6.	EDP Response Punch Card	184
A-7.	Electronic Data Card Survey Instrument	186

Preface

The purpose of this book is to provide investigators with a manageable set of guidelines and models which assist in the design of questionnaires, i.e., data-gathering instruments. Included is a brief description of how to conduct surveys. The major emphasis is placed on surveying as a decision-making process which aids in: (1) planning new programs, revising or improving current programs, or deleting obsolete programs; (2) determining the feelings, opinions, or attitudes of groups of individuals; (3) testing research hypotheses; and (4) contributing to educational theory. The author presents a spectrum of options ranging from the immediate and applied to the complex and theoretical.

Both uses and abuses of questionnaires and interviews are discussed. Models are included which illustrate how to construct and analyze both open-ended and forced-response items. Methods other than the typical questionnaire format, such as the Delphi technique, are also included.

Guidelines are presented for the design of questionnaires for those individuals who may not have access to specialists. It is assumed that the accompanying materials will be valuable to persons working on an independent basis and provide:

1. Checklists to evaluate questionnaire design for bias, objectivity, and workability.
2. Information on designing questions.
3. Methods for selecting sample populations and follow-up techniques.
4. Models which may be adapted.
5. Suggestions about analyzing data and communicating findings.

Acknowledgements

The user should consider this book as an introduction to data-gathering. The author prepared the text to be a helpful reference for both practitioners and students who desire to expand their own perspectives from a somewhat applied position.

Professors of educational research will find this book a welcome complement to the basic research methods text, as very few research texts dwell on surveys. Students are herein provided useful and thoughtful presentations which will improve their surveys markedly.

ACKNOWLEDGEMENTS

This book is made possible because of the combined efforts of many individuals. A very special acknowledgement goes to Patricia A. Clark, Nancy M. Fagan, and Gary A. Rust, who coauthored a research project manual from which this text evolved.

Lloyd B. Urdal gave an invaluable critique of the original draft. Gene Bigger's support and confidence is most sincerely acknowledged. Gratitude is also expressed to the many persons who have conducted surveys and shared their instruments with the author. A note of thanks is also given to Polly Gilkeson, Ann Moreland and Brenda Kelley who prepared the manuscipts.

Some of the material reported herein was initially prepared through a grant from the Research Coordinating Unit of the Washington State Commission for Vocational Education and the U.S. Office of Education. This book does not reflect the official position of either agency, only that of the author.

CHAPTER 1

Using a Survey to Collect Data

The decision to conduct a survey should be made after you have considered the alternatives. In far too many cases, persons conduct a survey to obtain data which could have been collected or abstracted from primary source reports, forms submitted to coordinating agencies, or other available records. Quite obviously, the use of mailed questionnaires is most widespread. A district superintendent of schools complained to the author that personnel in the central office completed an average of one questionnaire per day! If data-gathering instruments are used that widely, is it any wonder why so few returns ever approach 100 percent . . . or 70 percent . . . or 50 percent!

Thus, the first decision that you must make when designing a study, which could require a survey, is to determine if the data are already available at another source. If the response is in the negative, the next decision should address the questions of, "Is my survey really necessary?" "Will the information affect some policy?" "Will the information be used to expand educational theory?" Finally, ask yourself, "What is the problem or needs area on which my survey will focus?" When these questions have been answered, you are ready to plan for the conduct of a survey. Note well: The emphasis is on planning. And, it is that function which is emphasized in this book.

FOCUS

Surveys should focus on a selected problem, need, condition, or hypothetical proposition. The first task in conducting a survey is to determine what has already been written or published about the problem. This step is often called a "Review of the Literature." By conducting a thorough review of relevant published or unpublished reports and research, before you begin your survey, you will be able to determine: (1) if previous findings on the topic are useful to your focus; (2) if comparisons may be made with your anticipated groups and others; (3) if gaps exist in the reported information; (4) if some standardization of items may be necessary for comparative reasons; (5) if the selection of anticipated groups and sub-groups might need modifications; (6) if different techniques might be applied to your instrument or survey methodology; and (7) if a longitudinal study might be anticipated.

Surveys are often undertaken to determine the "state of the art" of some trait, trend, or program. Usually questionnaires are a part of the data-collection systems for these so-called status studies. One conducts a survey to determine, for example, the status of vocational tailoring, teacher preparation, or career education projects; how science is taught; attitudes of school board members or city council presidents; and a host of other subjects. If representative groups are surveyed, your studies could then be used as a base-line for future comparisons.

The important point that must be stressed is that surveys should always focus on some specific condition, state, need, problem, or hypothesis. A survey is designed to accomplish a specific purpose, which may be unique to a specific situation.

After you have identified a major focus or purpose and after you have conducted your review of the literature, you then list specific objectives which serve as the bases for the generation of specific questionnaire items.

For example, if you conclude <u>that it is necessary</u> to collect demographic data about the respondents, then your objectives might read:

1. An objective of this survey is to determine the age, sex, national origin, educational level, and current occupational status of each respondent.

Obviously plans must be made on the use of these demographic data at an early stage. Will you subdivide your responses by male-female divisions, or will age or occupation be used as an independent variable while the responses to other selected items become the dependent variables? These decisions must be made in the planning and designing stages of the survey so that you will not collect unnecessary information. Or, contrariwise, so that you will collect all the data which you need to complete a meaningful and valid analysis of responses. Further, by identifying your representative subgroups you may then test hypotheses or even generate hypotheses for long-range evaluations. With focus as a major point being emphasized, let us analyze the use of a printed questionnaire in data collection.

USING PRINTED INSTRUMENTS

The Questionnaire: Advantages and Disadvantages

Each questionnaire is constructed to address your established criteria or specific objectives. When designed and used in this manner, questionnaires are an efficient means by which to gather data. Many writers have commented on the advantages and disadvantages of the survey questionnaire. Below are discussed some commonly stated advantages and disadvantages of using questionnaires.

<u>General advantages</u>. The following list summarizes the overall general advantages of using a questionnaire to collect data.

1. Many individuals may be contacted at the same time, usually through the mail.
2. A questionnaire is less expensive to administer than is using an interview technique.
3. Each selected respondent receives identical questions.
4. A written questionnaire provides a vehicle for expression without fear of embarrassment to the respondent.
5. Responses are easily tabulated (depending on design of instrument).
6. Respondents may answer at their own convenience.
7. There is no need to select and train interviewers.
8. Persons in remote or distant areas are reached.
9. Interviewer biases are avoided.
10. Uniform data are gathered which allow for long-range research implications.

The above advantages must be carefully analyzed <u>for each specific survey</u>. Further, the timing of a survey is critical. Many school districts, for example have policies which specify that no one in the district is obliged to complete any questionnaire which has not been officially approved by the district. Additionally, the months of September, December, January, May, and June are very poor times in which to mail questionnaires. The months of July and August are most inappropriate for mailing questionnaires to school personnel since they are on vacation. Thus, a researcher should attempt to contact the intended respondents in October, November, February, March, and April. These months tend to be less busy for school personnel.

It might be most prudent to obtain a letter of endorsement from either a legal or extralegal association to enclose with your survey. Such endorsement informs the respondent that the survey is important. A survey that is to reach all members of a school unit, e.g., school district, should be endorsed by the district superintendent of schools or an authorized official. Perhaps you are surveying members of a specific extralegal group, e.g., members of a local or state teachers association, the school trustees in a region, or members of a professional association. In such cases, it is helpful to obtain a letter of endorsement from the association and include either a copy of the endorsing letter or a statement to that effect with the distributed instrument.

Your author has known of two state surveys which triggered adverse reactions from state leaders, who wrote their respective groups *not* to respond to surveys being conducted at the time. In both cases the number of returns was reduced substantially. Thus, if you have any reasonable concern about a negative influence, seek the endorsement of the group to improve the rate of your returns.

Timing (other than mailing) is also important to the survey. Often deadlines are being met and reports or recommendations based on the survey are promised to decision makers. In these situations detailed planning must be accomplished in advance of the actual conduct of the survey. One detailed plan is presented in Chapter 5, Figure 5-3.

As one example of needed planning and developing time, the author directed a rather short survey of vocational agricultural teacher supply and demand in Washington State. The instrument had only sixteen items. Yet, it took over six different drafts of the instrument and at least two months before all items were precisely stated and all focused on the problem. What took so long? Each draft was critiqued by persons not familiar with the survey and by the state leaders in the area of vocational agriculture. As criticisms arrived, the items were modified, deleted, or replaced and resubmitted to the group. This process took time, but the survey had been planned in advance to accommodate the time lag. The study apparently had widespread support, for a 97 percent return was obtained from 311 mailed!

All persons who conduct reputable surveys must take great care in item selection to eliminate any possible chance for unintended bias. This topic is discussed in Chapter 3 at great length. You may properly conclude that conducting a survey is a science, but it is also a careful blend of practical politics. Yet, do not infer that you must compromise your study or your ethics. The suggestion being offered here is that you need to realize that political factors may adversely affect the returns of your study. If you have any reasonable concern that some association or agency will attempt to adversely affect your returns, then incorporate that group in the early planning. After all, you might even convince the potential antagonists that your data will be helpful to them. Now let us focus on the opposing end of the spectrum.

Disadvantages of a questionnaire. For every advantage to conducting a questionnaire survey there is an accompanying disadvantage. A summary of disadvantages yields the following:
1. The investigator is prevented from learning the respondent's motivation for answering questions.
2. Respondents may be limited from providing free expression of opinions due to instrument design.
3. The collection of data from individuals who cannot read, write, or see is prevented.
4. The return of all questionnaires is difficult to achieve.
5. Complex designs cause poor responses or none.
6. The investigator is prevented from learning <u>what causes</u> poor returns.
7. The name and current addresses of the target population are often not available.
8. A question may have different meanings to different people.
9. There is no assurance that the intended respondent actually completes the instrument.
10. Selections of the sample, per se, may cause biased results: i.e., the sample is not representative of the universe.
11. The questionnaire asks for long outdated information.
12. Respondents may not complete the entire instrument.
13. Too much data are requested, thus, only an incomplete analysis is provided by the investigator.
14. Poor designs (open-ended questions) may lead to data that cannot be merged for the systematic analysis.
15. The topic is trite or simply insignificant.

The above list is far from complete but an investigator must realize the basic limitations of a written questionnaire. If the limitations do not render the survey void then a questionnaire may be used. Too, there are other concerns. For example, your author conducted a statewide survey; unknowingly, at the same time a similar survey was being circulated to the same target group. Undoubtedly, these two simultaneous surveys adversely affected the respective returns. It was both amusing and alarming (to me) to find that someone else's questionnaire had even been returned in our self-addressed, stamped envelope!

If a survey is required, but written questionnaires are not used, then what are the alternatives? There are two: personal interviews and telephone interviews.

TWO OTHER INFORMATION-COLLECTING TECHNIQUES

The Interview: Advantages and Disadvantages

Personal interviews are a means of collecting data or information. What are some of the common characteristics concerning personal interviews? One of the most favorable aspects is the interviewer's personal contact with the respondents. In this setting, one can clarify any question immediately. A generalized set of advantages about interviews show that:

1. Feelings of the respondents are revealed.
2. Discussion is allowed about the causes of problems or solutions to problems.
3. The respondent is allowed maximum opportunity for free expression.
4. The interviewer can observe and tabulate nonverbal behaviors.
5. Respondents may provide personal information, attitudes, beliefs, and perceptions that might not be gained on a written instrument.
6. A high rate of participation is provided.
7. The interviewer has an opportunity to follow-up or probe for leads.
8. Individuals who cannot read, write, or see can participate.

9. Fewer individuals may be needed than for mailed surveys.

10. Comparisons may be made with mailed surveys.

A survey conducted by interview takes much longer to complete than a comparable questionnaire survey, but the informants (respondents) tend to comply, usually assuring a 100% response rate. One major consideration is how to record information during an interview. An interviewer may use a tape recorder, or write verbatim as the interview takes place. Some informants will not allow an interviewer to tape record, while others get nervous about written notes taken during the conversation. This is one aspect of an interview that cannot be predicted in advance. The interviewer should ask the informant if the interview may be tape recorded or if taking notes would be allowed. The interviewer might even tell the informant that the responses which are recorded may be reviewed by the informant for editing or other comments. Interviews are used to determine attitudes or opinions. Yet, discretion must be exercised lest overly sensitive questions be introduced which alienate informants.

If the size of the representative sample group is comparatively small, then an interview technique would be most appropriate, or, even the telephone interview which will be discussed later in the chapter. Yet, if the informants are scattered throughout a region or state the cost to conduct personal interviews could be exorbitant.

<u>Interview types</u>. As with questionnaires there are two general types of interviews: directed and nondirected. The directed interview is highly structured. An interview schedule or guide is prepared in advance. A nondirected or unstructured interview is not tightly structured with a

specifically prepared interview schedule as is the directed type.
When using unstructured designs, the interviewer identifies a basic
topic and then probes into areas which seem fruitful to explore. A
structured interview specifies an identical set of questions to be
answered by all. The unstructured interview may not specify an identical
schedule although common items can be used. Thus, there may be the
problem of arriving at a consensus or set of generalizations from the sample
where totally unstructured interviews are used.

Conducting an interview. Regardless of the type of interview used,
some plan is required. The plan is usually structured and lists the
questions to be asked in a sequence or order. This plan and any
alternatives are called the "interview schedule." Generally, an interviewer
begins with a series of structured and perhaps simple fact questions.
These are usually nonthreatening questions which help the informant to
"loosen up." After the initial items, more pressing or feeling-types of
questions are asked.

Even if only one person conducts the interviews, detailed training
sessions must be conducted. All interviewers must be trained to avoid
interjecting bias in the questions through verbal or nonverbal reactions
during the interview. If one person does the interviewing, then it is
essential to practice several trial interviews. If possible, use videotape
during the trials to determine if the interview sessions are nonbiased
and are appropriately conducted.

In some cases it might be essential that interviews be scheduled via
an appointment with the informant. In these cases, the informant's
schedule will take precedence over the interviewer's. When appointments are

made, explain the objective of the interview and then set an appointment. Be prepared to spend a greater amount of time with each informant than you initially plan. As with questionnaires, cover letters explain why you are there and that all responses will be treated confidentially. These same points are verbalized in an interview. However, many interviews are probably not scheduled in advance.

Disadvantages. The interview is usually more expensive than a mailed survey for three reasons: training, transportation, and wages. Major disadvantages of the interview technique include the following points:

1. The method is time-consuming.
2. Only a limited number of persons may be interviewed due to time and cost.
3. Quantification of results may be difficult for unstructured interviews.
4. Scheduling of interviews may be difficult.
5. Costs may be prohibitive.
6. Respondents might feel that they are being "put on the spot."
7. The interviewer may make subjective judgments about the responses, and thus bias the data.
8. The overall reliability of responses can be limited since respondents tend to answer truthfully those questions which are not embarrassing to them.
9. Interview responses are sometimes biased depending upon the age, sex, education, race, interview experience, socio-economic level, and religious background of the interviewer.

The criteria for any survey will in part play a deciding role in the determination of whether or not to conduct interviews. If the advantages of an interview are greater than those of a mailed questionnaire, the interview tends to be a very revealing technique.

Telephone Interviews

Telephone interviews provide an effective survey method. The same general contraints and rules apply to telephone interviews as apply to personal interviews. However, in telephone interviews the structured schedule may be preferable to the unstructured since people tend to consider telephone conversations as somewhat privileged.

Telephone interviews may be conducted via long distance, which reduces travel costs. Interviews conducted over the telephone will be highly reliable, if the interview schedule is nonbiased. Persons respond freely to telephone surveys once initial rapport and trust have been established. Telephone interviewing is a very effective method, especially when seeking opinions on issues relating to public policy. Of course, a structured interview is easier to conduct and less expensive than is an unstructured one. The schedule which follows provides some ideas on how to proceed in the conduct of any interview.

To be certain, caution must be exercised when using a telephone survey to avoid the bias of <u>noninclusion</u>. Any sample may be very biased by not selecting a <u>representative</u> group of the universe or population. Such caveats are most serious when sampling persons from lower socioeconomic groups, migratory groups, or those who tend to move frequently, e.g., construction workers. Obviously, the personal interview would be the more appropriate technique for such individuals. However, if a rather homogeneous group is to be polled, then the telephone survey may be a highly productive method. Homogeneous groups are defined as those groups of individuals who tend to share common or distinguishing traits. Examples of homogeneous groups would be: superintendents of schools, elementary school principals, lunch room supervisors, insurance salespersons, grocery store checkers, to list but a few. With such groups telephone interviews would prove to be most reliable and valid.

The Interview Schedule

The plan or outline to be used when conducting the interview is the "schedule." As stated before, the schedule assists the interviewer to remain on "task" and helps ensure that all informants have an opportunity to respond to the identical phrasing of a particular question.

A point to remember when designing the interview schedule is to avoid questions that can be answered with a "Yes" or "No" response. One purpose of an interview is to gather perceptions which are unique to the informant. Also, avoid language that might be considered offensive by the respondent.

One type of question that the interview schedule might contain is one that does provide some factual data, such as:

"How long have you lived in this city?"

After a few of these "easies," lead into more open-ended questions that provide subjective data from the informant such as:

"To what extent do you think that the present vocational education program at the high school is meeting the needs of our youth?"

The interviewer must decide whether to record responses during the interview or immediately after the interview. It is recommended that the interviewer concentrate on what the respondent is actually saying. This takes a great deal of practice if accuracy is to be maintained. If delayed recording of informant responses is used, they must be written down immediately following the interview so that the context and main points are not forgotten. In such cases, be prepared in advance with a pre-made check list-- paper remembers best.

It is suggested that all interviewers be trained in the processes of translating information before they ever interview the selected sample respondents. Such training would help to alleviate the unconscious interjection of biased interpretations or totally incorrect statements.

Lest an incorrect perception be made, interviews also use very carefully constructed questions with forced responses. The interview schedules used for this design closely resemble any forced-response questionnaire. The formats illustrated later in Chapters 2, 3, and 6 could be adapted with great ease to interview schedules. The format which follows could be used when constructing a structured interview schedule, or could be modified to represent a forced-response model.

Model 1-1. One Type of Interview Schedule

PARENT INTERVIEW

Name_____ Date_____

Address_____ Time_____

_____

1. How long have you lived in this city?
2. Where did you attend high school?
3. How many of your children attend high school in this city?
4. What type of vocational education courses should be provided for high school students?
5. What type of vocational education courses should not be provided for high school students?
6. What changes would you like to see in the present high school vocational education program?
7. Describe the types of vocational skills you feel should be taught in a high school vocational education program.

Observe in the above schedule that items 4-7 could be interchanged by the interviewer. In a structured interview, the interviewer would proceed through a definite list of items, just as one completes a questionnaire. When using an unstructured technique the interviewer may probe for additional comments or may alter the sequences of the planned set of questions. It should be noted that probing is also permitted with structured interviews. Both techniques require training and should be used only after such training since it is rather easy to "lead" respondents to make statements which project the desires of the interviewer--not the informant!

ADDITIONAL GUIDELINES TO DETERMINE SURVEY USE

An important planning consideration for the type of survey, either questionnaire or interview, concerns budget limitations. It is crucial to project realistic cost analyses for the following major tasks or elements:

1. Printing costs of the questionnaire, cover letter, or special forms.
2. Mailing and follow-up costs.
3. Typing of original and revised questionnaires after field testing.
4. Editing, marking, and tabulating returned questionnaires.
5. Estimating the electronic data processing needs, if required, including key punch and machine time.
6. Identifying needed office supplies.
7. Computing additional or part-time staff wages.
8. Training costs for interviewers.
9. Researching cost for review of the literature.
10. Estimating telephone needs.
11. Preparing the final report.

Costs of mailed surveys are similar to those of the personal interview, except the postage cost will be replaced by the interviewer cost, including the training of the interviewers and the actual cost for the field test of the interview instrument. To aid in planning the costs of a survey, a somewhat realistic example is presented below.

Sample Survey Budget

The following budget figures are for illustrative purposes only. Actual cost figures may vary a great deal from those figures shown below due to fluctuating economic and regional conditions.

<u>Wages</u>. Plan to spend no less than $3.00 per hour for clerical help. It may be prudent to retain part-time staff persons (four hours a day) for at least four weeks for the simplest survey, at a total cost of $240.00. This item may be excluded from your budget by investigating the use of educational aides already employed by your school. In addition, you might request assistance from business students through a course instructor. Consultant fees vary from no cost to over $300.00 a day. If consultants are required, be certain to determine and plan for their costs.

<u>Services</u>. There are many variables associated with electronic data processing. This budget item can be determined by asking computer specialists for cost estimates. If you have about 400 respondents, and a rather uncomplicated survey, a $400.00 budget would probably be adequate. But, the more complex the analyses, the greater the cost.

<u>Materials</u>. Cost of materials varies, depending on the source of supplies. Paper and office supplies must be estimated. Although the estimated budget will vary with each mailed survey, typically it costs between

$1.00 and $2.00 per respondent for the materials, printing, and mailing of a questionnaire which includes a self-addressed envelope. Additional postage costs must be calculated for follow-ups. For the first follow-up a postcard is usually used. A second follow-up, if required (and it almost always is), would include a letter and possibly another questionnaire. It is recommended that a third follow-up be conducted to yield a higher rate of return.

Training costs. If individuals must be trained to work on the survey, to make personal contacts, or to conduct telephone surveys, then a systematic training program must be instituted to insure that all interviewers or survey workers meet a minimum criterion level of demonstrated competence. As survey director you must establish a performance checklist of all desired interview behaviors: establishing rapport, asking questions, recording data, remaining objective in verbal and nonverbal cues, being nonjudgmental when probing, observing, summarizing objectively, to list a few important ones.

One training technique that will be most effective is to use videotaped training episodes. A structured set of training episodes may be designed with each being planned to provide the appropriate behaviors for the trainees. A most powerful training technique is first to provide an appropriate model of the behavior. The trainee observes the model, then practices the specific behavior with another individual (it could be another trainee). All episodes are videotaped and immediately critiqued. All trainees continue through the training sequence until all prescribed behaviors are correctly emitted, or until they meet preestablished criterion measures. Such a program would require that a budget be estimated to include trainee time costs, plus rental of videotape equipment--if not available.

As you might conclude, conducting a survey must be approached as one aspect of the research business. The budget for a rather limited survey may easily surpass $1,000 when one must pay for part-time help and data processing.

A similar and limited interview design could exceed $8,000 or $10,000. Budget considerations may well determine if, in fact, you will even conduct the study.

This chapter has presented a few general aspects that are important to your decision to conduct a survey. Once the decision is made to conduct a questionnaire survey, then the writing of the questions becomes critical. That topic is the focus of Chapter 2.

CHAPTER 2

Designing the Items

PLANNING FOR ITEM CONSTRUCTION

Identifying the questionnaire format, then writing appropriate and carefully formulated questions for the instrument may be the single most important and time consuming task of conducting a survey. The construction of each item determines whether or not the survey will elicit the desired information. Instrument format closely follows the types of items for questions to be generated. If you decide to use a forced-response format, then all items must be adapted to coincide with that mode. Format and item construction should be determined early in your planning so that your efforts are efficiently utilized.

All design efforts must focus on your expressed purpose and the written specific objectives pertaining to the survey. By stating your purpose and the informational objectives, item construction becomes a set of tasks which should illustrate consistent and logical interfaces. <u>All</u> items must relate to the purpose or objectives or they should not be used. It is not uncommon to observe questionnaires with excessive items, which in turn are never reported by the investigator. One exception might be the initial survey conducted for a longitudinal study, where some items will be reported or compared in the future. Most surveys, however, are simply "one-shot" exercises and should be kept closely in focus.

You establish the criteria for the content. After items are generated you should then analyze your items against the criteria discussed below. Such analysis is, in one sense, the measure of internal validity.

Parsimony

Ask only for information which cannot be obtained elsewhere. Questions that are nice to know or might be useful for another study lengthen the questionnaire and may threaten the credibility of the study. Selecting appropriate questions depends on having precisely formulated objectives for the survey. Plan in advance how the information from each question will be used in the final report.

Surveys taken in schools, for example, frequently ask a number of objective questions such as respondent's age, sex, parents' occupations, major in school, and address, "for possible use at some later date." Caution should be exercised when obtaining addresses for follow-up studies. The U.S. Bureau of the Census has observed that between 15 and 18 percent of the addresses of individuals change each year. Address information may be obsolete before you ever use it again, so carefully consider this need. If the information is not needed for the intended study, do not request it. Sensitive questions, such as a respondent's values, should definitely be avoided if the information does not relate directly to some variable.

It may be possible to ask a related question to obtain the desired information. For example, if it is essential to know the respondent's income, ask each respondent for the respondent's occupation and then approximate the income by checking local occupational salary averages available from the U.S. Bureau of the Census or local Employment Security Offices. Or, as will be illustrated later, establish a continuum of salary data for selection.

When seemingly unnecessary or sensitive questions are included in a survey, a typical participant reaction is to "throw the whole thing away." Only one or two inappropriate questions can destroy your credibility and reduce the response rate. Do not conclude that questionnaires can only be a few items in length. Length is often immaterial to success. The point being stressed here is "necessity."

Specificity

Questions which are too general can only lead to overly generalized conclusions--which may not be very important. If more than one aspect of a topic is addressed in a single question, the question will be ambiguous. Thus, you may need to create several items which will add specificity to the responses. The following exemplify survey questions which need improvement. The illustration which follows shows how the question can be improved.

1. Do you think that science should be taught in elementary school?

    ( ) Yes
    ( ) No
    ( ) No Opinion

The question as stated is far too general. In this example the investigator has assumed that the respondents "know" which grades are encompassed in an elementary school--K-4, K-7, K-8, K-9? A specific limit should be concisely stated. For example:

2. In which grades would you favor the teaching of science?

    ( ) Grades kindergarten to three
    ( ) Grades four to eight
    ( ) Grades seven and eight
    ( ) All grades, kindergarten through eight
    ( ) No science should be taught in these grades

Observe how item 2 subdivides the grade areas into defined units.

Another technique might be to ask an open-ended question, "In which grade should science instruction be initiated in our elementary schools?" Each respondent could then state a grade. However, there is a very high probability that you will receive such a wide variety of responses that the item might not show any trend. By using a forced-response continuum, respondent trends can be more quantitatively observed.

3. Are you in favor of science instruction in grades K-8?

( ) Yes
( ) No
( ) No opinion

This question is too vague. The word "favor" will be subjectively defined by each respondent. A more specific question would produce more usable data. Again, as written, a respondent may favor science for one or more grades, but not others, and thus, in the above might simply check "No."

4. Should schools offer science instruction in grades K-8?

( ) Yes
( ) No
( ) No opinion

Observe that a respondent may respond by checking "Yes" but yet have no intention of supporting such a course in the local school. The question asked covers an "impersonal" connotation. It does not explicitly ask whether "our schools," or the schools of "X District," or even the specific schools of a city should have science instruction. If the purpose of the questi is to assess the desirability for a course, then ask the respondent an explicit question to that effect. Never construct items which are open to varying interpretations by the respondents or the investigators.

5. What is your favorite subject? _____

The results from this question may indicate little or no generalizable results, or at best results which are inconclusive. A more reasonable approach would be to have each respondent rank-order a series of various clusters of subjects. Yet, favorite subjects may not be the subjects which a person values most. Every word in every item must be carefully selected to coincide with the purpose of the study. To avoid biasing the items, analyze each item by asking yourself, "Is this item explicit or implicit?" If the latter, then rewrite the item.

6. What vocational courses would you like added to the list of offerings in our high school? _____

In this case, more additional information must be provided to the respondent, such as the current listing of vocational courses. In that manner the question can be more precisely addressed, with the responses being assessed for trends. As written above, question 6 should also be accompanied by another question requesting information about future plans to attend college, since college-bound students may respond with "none." Further, students entering science or engineering related courses in universities might find industrial arts or vocational offerings relevant to their future needs. Thus, a series of questions might be developed which specifically focuses on their opinions.

7. How many hours do you usually work each week? _____

Seasonal workers, such as some construction workers, and a professor or two may respond to this question: "60 hours per week." To get an accurate calculation of actual working time, a question must also be asked that will reveal the length of the usual work and layoff periods. If question 7 were asked of any group the results would be chaotic since the question is too vague and has no reference point.

To avoid being redundant, the examples relating to specificity seem adequate enough. The rationale for designing very specific questions is related to the degree to which the collected data are explicit or implicit. Explicitly designed items will yield generalizations that are supported by data, while implicitly designed items are open to many interpretations--often the data will not support implied conclusions when questionnaires are used. A general rule to follow when generating items is to be as specific as possible.

Respondents' Knowledge

A major factor to anticipate in survey design relates to the criterion, "Do the selected subjects possess enough information to respond rationally?" Occasionally, questions are asked of individuals who do not have adequate information to make a rational response. Allow for this situation by providing nonvalue choices such as "Do not know" or "No opinion." However, if the nonvalue responses are marked frequently, the wrong group may have been surveyed or the worng question may have been asked. For example, it would be of little value to poll public opinion concerning the adequacy of a school's insurance coverage. Probably most people have no knowledge that such a policy even exists. This topic will be further addressed in Chapter 7.

The criterion of having an adequate data base from which to respond is critical in school related surveys. Surveys in education tend to use "esoteric lexicons"--jargon and technical terminology that may be known by its practitioners, but not by citizens at large. Further, by using undefined concepts such as "accountability," "career education," "team teaching," "homogeneous grouping," or "year-round schools" in educational surveys focused on the general populace, one might be inviting scorn from the respondents. One school district recently asked a series of questions of its patrons which brought a public retort in the local newspaper about poor item design, biases, and the inappropriateness of the survey. The returns to that survey were very poor--the interpretations proved to be less than desirable.

Questionnaires are not designed to instruct the respondents about issues, techniques or problems. They are designed to gather opinions or attitudes about already known issues, problems, or events. If you are attempting to gather opinions about some new educational innovations, e.g., computer assisted instruction, you may desire to focus on other specific attendant issues--time at terminals, independent study, varying individual schedules--not on professional issues which require a great deal of knowledge about computer aided instruction.

Interest

Consideration must also be given to the potential for respondents' interest in the topic. If the general interest in the survey topic is low, then completed returns may be rather low. One means by which to increase interest in a questionnaire is to send out a "prequestionnaire" letter telling the participants about its forthcoming delivery. Another technique is to create items designed specifically for each identified subgroup. By using this technique a questionnaire is directed toward a specific subgroup of respondents, e.g., students, business and professional persons, patrons, teachers, or administrators. Designing and constructing separate questionnaires for each selected group will thereby obtain different perceptions.

For example, to evaluate the potential for success of anticipated course offerings, students might be polled to assess their attitude toward enrolling in a particular class. School patrons are usually polled if the program is a major departure from the usual operations. When planning a survey, attempt to address all relevantly concerned groups so that the studies collectively complement each other. Such a model is typically used in the conduct of the so-called "needs" assessments, which most governmental units conduct on regularly scheduled bases, especially public school districts.

Do not hesitate to use surveys to determine attitudes or opinions about highly provocative topics. These studies generally lead to very high response rates. The major problem in conducting a survey on such topics is that they may be too emotion-laden, so great care must be exercised to construct a most objective instrument, addressing the issues in an impartial manner.

Single Variable Items

One criterion that is often violated in item construction concerns the specifying of only one variable, trait, or event per individual item. Examine the following statement taken from a doctoral study, mailed questionnaire:

8. With respect to your present position and responsibilities, how do you feel your doctoral program prepared you for the situation in which you are working and the problems you face? (check one)

___Very adequately   ___Adequately   ___Very inadequately

Comment: _____

Observe how the writer of that item combines situation <u>and</u> problems in one category. These are definitely two traits and should have been separated. The three forced responses are biased to the positive. If respondents simply checked one of the three at random, there would be a 67 percent positive response rate. Finally, the writer was apparently unaware of the concept of upward job mobility. People are promoted, move to new challenges, seek out more creative environments or seek leadership positions. Such well-known job traits demonstrate an inferred naiveté of the researcher in item construction. You only need one item such as the above illustration to raise the ire of respondents to retort with angry letters--or simply to throw the instrument away: Or, to save them for illustrations in books!

The combination of two or more mutually exclusive items is a very common error in logic and item construction. If two traits are to be addressed, then use two different statements. The "tip-off" of an inappropriate statement is the inclusion of a conjunction--and, but, or--in a statement. Precision in wording and thought is an imperative. Or, if a "doublet" happens to be inserted into an instrument, that statement is considered "null and void" in the tabulations. As a surveyor you are absolutely not allowed to speculate on the respondents' motives, probable intent, or likely response. In an earlier section, it was cautioned to construct all items in an explicit manner. The interpretations of explicit data will be objective, whereas all implicitly derived interpretations must be considered subjective or projective and are not allowable. The latter in a survey illustrates nothing more than an opinion of the investigator. It also implies sloppiness and the possibility of a biased and, therefore, an invalid study.

Keep your statements simple, explicit, and singular.

Simplicity

Can the question be misunderstood? Again, beware of using complex terminology when conducting surveys. Terms such as "closed campus" or "module" may mean nothing to some and too many things to others. Educators are frequently insensitive to the jargon and concepts which they use. Most educational terms are totally unknown or misunderstood by school patrons. Language and vocabulary limitations of the clientele are important considerations that must be realized when developing a survey instrument Words that have multiple or vague definitions may invalidate the entire questionnaire.

As you construct your questionnaire items, choose synonyms which both connote and denote precise terms or concepts. Do not attempt to "dazzle" the respondents with polysyllabic words or long, complex sentences. Absolutely avoid statements with "catch" dependent clauses. A questionnaire to be administered to school-aged populations should be tested by one of the many readability formulas to determine the approximate grade reading level of each item. The lack of definition of key words causes pupils to misconstrue your statements--and probably provides you with invalid data. If there are doubts about the wording of a question, write it in different ways and field test the questions on a small subgroup to determine which version elicits the data in the desired form. Better yet, provide a series of forced-response or rank order items to judge the quality of the item. It is also recommended that "debriefings" be held with field test group members. This means that you interview each person as the draft versions are completed. Terms which are too difficult or unclear should be identified so that appropriate vocabulary may be substituted.

Sensitive Areas

Topics such as age, income, religion, values, personal habits, and personal likes, dislikes, and sexually related activities are usually classified as "sensitive." These topics are _not_ taboos, but must be addressed by very discreet means. In some cases your intended questionnaire may be judged as an "invasion of privacy." The topic of protection of individuals is addressed in Chapter 5. If you have any question about whether your questionnaire violates either legal or ethical canons, seek the counsel of any state or private university graduate school dean who is involved in research. All such institutions must, by Federal Regulation, have an established committee to review all projects which "involve human subjects."

For the purpose of this book, the concept of sensitivity will also focus on the careful selection of words and phrases. Terms such as "school dropout" and "poor grades" can be offensive and should not be used. Respondents tend to avoid questions which show them in adverse perspectives. Terms such as these should be omitted if possible, but if the information is necessary, word the question to make the topic less offensive or at least "neutral" in value connotation and denotation. Examine the next two examples.

9. How old are you? _____

Students may not object to this question, but the general public may. Sensitive information of this character may be obtained by using a response continuum with five-year or ten-year intervals. It is less offensive for the respondent to put a check mark in the 35-39 category than it is to write 39 years of age.

10. Do you have a discipline problem in your classes?
    ( ) Yes
    ( ) No
    ( ) No opinion

The results from this question will invariably be less than accurate because the respondent may not be aware or may not desire to admit that a discipline problem exists. This information can be obtained more accurately be asking questions such as, "Over the last five school days, have you had a child disrupt your class to the point where punitive action was necessary: e.g., sent to office or being sent out of the room?" "If yes, how many children?" A teacher who sends four or five students out of the room in a week's time may be defined by the researcher as having a discipline problem. By asking situational questions, the term "discipline problem" is more operationally defined. Comparisons can then be made with other respondents.

Another technique for eliciting data about "discipline" problems is to arrange a list of anticipated responses. From such a listing, one-shot, short-term, or longitudinal data may be collected. Observe the item below.

11. Every teacher has some problem in classroom management. Below are a series of techniques that teachers have used in managing inappropriate pupil behaviors. Please check those techniques which you have used during the five-day school week which just ended.

    ___ Detention after school
    ___ Expulsion was recommended
    ___ Extra class assignments
    ___ Isolation of individual from class group
    ___ Nonverbal facial or body language expressed by teacher
    ___ Note sent home to parents
    ___ Recess privileges withheld
    ___ Reduction of grade on classwork
    ___ Sent to "office"
    ___ Suspended from class
    ___ Verbal reprimand made
    ___ Work task assigned

The above would provide an indicator of use. You could repeat the list asking how many pupils were actually involved in each technique for a specified period of time. The time dimension is important if you are to determine some relative index for comparative purposes. If racial or sexual bias is suspected add those dimensions as separate items.

When attempting to collect data which may be categorized as "sensitive" you always run the risk of causing some ire to a small group or, perhaps the entire group of respondents. What has been offered here is a mechanism which stresses writing style, word selection, and technique to accomplish the task of obtaining relevant and accurate, yet sensitive, data.

Semantics of Construction

There have been a number of studies on the personal and impersonal wording of questionnaries. These show that results do differ with just a slight change in the wording in this regard. Versions of personal and impersonal questions follow.

12. To what extent are reference materials in the library satisfactory?

    ( ) Very satisfactory
    ( ) Satisfactory
    ( ) No opinion
    ( ) Unsatisfactory
    ( ) Very unsatisfactory

13. To what extent do you think that reference materials in the library are satisfactory?

    ( ) Very satisfactory
    ( ) Satisfactory
    ( ) No opinion
    ( ) Unsatisfactory
    ( ) Very unsatisfactory

When answering question number 12, the respondent may consider other teachers' and persons' opinions along with his or her own. Question number 13 specifically asks for a personal response. Use personal or impersonal wording to elicit the response appropriate to the purpose of the study.

There are no definite rules for deciding whether to use a personal or an impersonal style. Each specific survey must be analyzed by the researcher. Consider each question individually when making decisions--by focusing on sensitive topics, personal attitudes versus public attitudes, and respondent background.

There is a tendency for a respondent to identify more closely with an item when it is written in a personal style. All reference points are from an individual perspective. The interpretations of the responses can be more conclusive since there is a high degree of explicitness. Contrariwise, impersonal wording tends to reduce the onus of individual responsibility and allows a respondent to be involved in the situation, but not personally identified with it. Observe how questions can be written to accomodate the two styles.

14. Why were you fired? _____

15. How would you rate your relationships with your managers?

   ( ) Very good
   ( ) Good
   ( ) Sometimes good, sometimes poor
   ( ) Poor
   ( ) Very poor

16. What percentage of employees tend not to get along well with others?

   ( ) 100%
   ( ) More than 50%
   ( ) About 50%
   ( ) Less than 50%
   ( ) None

17. How is the work rated by managers?

   ( ) Very good
   ( ) Good
   ( ) Sometimes good, sometimes poor
   ( ) Poor
   ( ) Very poor

Question 14 and the three subsequent questions could be designed for the purpose of ascertaining the reasons why people are dismissed from their jobs. The questionnaires using a personal approach in questions 14 and 15 may probably not be returned or will be vaguely or perhaps dishonestly answered. By asking impersonal questions, such as items 16 and 17, more accurate and more precise information can be obtained.

A well-constructed set of impersonal questions will provide data from which a set of logical inferences may be drawn. But caution must be employed; the inferences are more projective than they are explicit. Any conclusions from such a technique must be held very tentatively until more explicit data are obtained.

The entire questionnaire must be concisely written so that the respondent is not required to use time "guessing" about question intent. To insure accuracy and ease in responding, questions should be arranged in a sequential manner. For example, if the question below were the only one asked the results could be very erroneous.

18. Do you plan to enroll in a vocational school after high school graduation?

    ( ) Yes
    ( ) No
    ( ) Do not know

This type of question could be used to separate respondents into subgroups. Those respondents who answered positively could be requested to answer a set of items designed particularly for them, and a similar provision could be made for the negative respondents.

19. Would you like to see a course on "Family and Child Care" returned to the high school's curriculum?

    ( ) Yes
    ( ) No
    ( ) No opinion

The word "returned" indicates the course had been offered previously, but dropped for some reason. If two or three years had passed, it cannot

be assumed that teachers, students, and parents will remember the course.
A brief description of the course should be given and the word "returned"
should then be clarified by stating when and perhaps why the course was
dropped.

   20. Have you ever had the opportunity to use your mathematics training
       after graduation.

       ( ) Yes
       ( ) No
       ( ) I did not take any mathematics

The background of each respondent is important in obtaining valid
information from this question. When polling the sample, persons with
mathematics experience must be separated from those with none. In this manner,
the response can be better interpreted by subgroup analysis. However, question
number 20 is a very poor one. What is meant by "ever used?" There are
simply too many interpretations to the question. If the question is needed,
reword an entire series of questions which identify clusters of skills
associated with those taught in mathematics.

The examples above are provided to alert you to the problems of
interpretation which are so closely associated with the semantics of
questionnaire construction. As the item constructor, you may be unaware of
the connotations. Yet, to avoid the building of inadvertent biases or errors,
you must examine every word to be certain that it precisely conveys the
meaning that you intend. Outside reviewers are most helpful for the
identification of any semantic problems.

Manageability

When constructing questionnaires you must also plan to make the completing of the instrument efficient and manageable for the participant. Respondents are giving their own time and effort to provide you with information, otherwise not available. Therefore, design your instrument to be efficient and easy to use. Lengthy questionnaires with too many specific items may cause loss of interest, create confusion, or prevent the completion of the instrument. Do not overwhelm respondents with organizational complexities when constructing a questionnaire. Questionnaires are almost always completed on a volunteer basis-- to be done in a very quick, even cursory manner--so construct simple, uncomplicated instruments.

A list of fifty items that requires respondents to check the ones of interest to them is a confusing and boring task. A better method would be to group the items into a series of logical categories and ask for preferences within specific groupings.

When respondents are asked to rank a list of items, the list should not contain more than ten items. Lists over ten become rather difficult to judge. Most people are not generally willing to take the time and effort needed to complete one set of extensive rankings with any great care. It is better to compile two or more shorter lists. The respondents would then be asked to rank order each list. In general, one ought to consider five or six items as an optimum number to rank order for any specific set.

Avoiding Bias

Researchers often hold preconceived conclusions or assumptions pertaining to the topic, respondents, or hypothesized results. These assumptions can cause a "bias" to be built into a survey instrument. Such biases and nonrepresentative sampling almost always yield biased or unreliable results. Investigators with a vested interest in a survey must be cautioned not to "load" a questionnaire by favoring one side of an issue or by devising questions which force respondent bias. Loading a questionnaire in any manner does not allow respondents the opportunity to disclose their true opinions about an issue. <u>Any deliberate loading or biasing is totally unethical and unprofessional</u>. It is also professionally dangerous: you'll probably be caught and discredited!

Many educators study the topic of innovations, diffusion of innovations, and implementation strategies. If you decided to assess techniques used by school leaders to locate high school curricula innovations, a questionnaire might be used, with one item asking:

21. Which of the following sources do you use for locating information about new high school curricula? (You may check more than one source.)

    ( ) 21.1 State Department of Education personnel
    ( ) 21.2 Professional associates
    ( ) 21.3 Professional journals
    ( ) 21.4 Local school district consultants
    ( ) 21.5 Regional research laboratories
    ( ) 21.6 Book company sales representatives
    ( ) 21.7 Other (please specify) _____

The built-in bias or probable assumption is that the respondents are now seeking information. If a number of respondents check only one item, that item may lead to the unwarranted conclusion that respondents are unaware of leads to useful sources of information. However, some of the polled leaders may not actively seek information sources; therefore, sources about curricula may be known but are not being utilized.

In this case, to assess the knowledge about information seeking rather than the actual behavior, the item could be rewritten as is illustrated below, or, both items could be used to clarify the point.

    22. If you wanted to locate information about new high school curricula, which of the following sources would you use? (Check any number that you would use.)

        ( ) 22.1 State Department of Education personnel
        ( ) 22.2 Professional associates
        ( ) 22.3 Professional journals
        ( ) 22.4 Local school district consultants
        ( ) 22.5 Regional research laboratories
        ( ) 22.6 Book company sales representatives
        ( ) 22.7 Other (please specify) _____

The item above places all respondents into a neutral frame of reference which seeks respondent possible activity. Unwarranted assumptions about the respondents are avoided in this manner. The framing of questions may reflect assumptions about respondents which may introduce unrecognized bias.

One ought to be aware of another rather subtle bias that can be built into an instrument--the "yes tendency," or the "response pattern syndrome." While responding to a list of questions, respondents may inadvertently develop "mind set" by continuously answering in only one direction. This tendency can be partially offset by including inverse or reverse questions. This question-constructing technique requires the use of pairs scattered throughout the questionnaire. The technique helps to avoid the "yes tendency" and also acts as a means of checking respondent consistency on some issue or point.

Questions that are direct opposites to others tend to be redundant, but related ideas can be used to construct reversely constructed questions. The following pair of questions might be used in determining attitudes toward a longer school year.

23. Do you favor a school year longer than our present nine months?

    ( ) 23.1 Yes
    ( ) 23.2 No
    ( ) 23.3 Undecided

24. If the school board approved a school year shorter than our present nine month plan would you endorse such a decision?

    ( ) 24.1 Yes
    ( ) 24.2 No
    ( ) 24.3 Undecided

In the above set, if "yes" were marked for both questions, one could conclude that the respondent fell into a "yes tendency" or that the respondent is inconsistent in opinion. A field test of a questionnaire may identify items that cause a "yes tendency." The researcher may then make adjustments for its reduction. Obviously, questions such as 23 and 24 are separated in the questionnaire and would not follow each other. This technique is useful when policy issues are being analyzed.

Positive Wording

Several years ago one of the Hit Parade songs was "Accentuate the Positive." The same logic is applied to the constructing of questionnaire items. All statements should be written as positive statements. In absolutely all cases <u>never</u> use double negative construction or future conditional items. Examine the two "negative" models below and then ask yourself if they meet the criteria listed previously.

25. Would you not support the establishment of a regional center?

26. Even though you responded in the negative to item 25, if the regional center were established, to what extent would you support it?

Negative items cause confusion for the respondent. The use of speculative items provides spurious data at best. Further, such speculative data are usually predicated on varying conditions which may allow investigator bias to enter.

The two previous examples should have been written as:

27. To what extent would you support the establishment of a regional center?

Item 27 is simple, straightforward and positive. The respondent then has the option to select from a continuum of positive or negative reactions.

ITEM SEQUENCING

By using the eleven general criteria for item construction--parsimony, specificity, respondents' knowledge, interest, single variable items, simplicity, sensitive areas, semantics of construction, manageability, positive wording, and avoiding bias--as a checklist, the specification of your items will be substantially improved. The next major task is to place or sequence the items in a logical or consistent pattern.

Logical Leads

Question placement is very important since the respondent must usually recall information, form opinions, or perhaps respond to some items which may be personal, e.g., age, schooling, values. The questionnaire should reflect a well-organized outline, with each set of items addressing a distinct topic. In this manner respondents tend to react positively to the behavior of responding.

When seeking chronological information, arrange the items so that the respondent begins with the present. For example, if one were seeking an employment profile the question might ask: "List the jobs which you have held chronologically, beginning with your present one." If such an item were to be a chief source of information, then the investigator might prepare a form which listed job categories, dates begun, dates quit, and other relevant descriptions.

When sensitive areas are assessed, it is important that a conducive "psychological set" be established. If school "dropouts" are initially asked, "Why did you quit high school?" the few responses that might be returned will probably be vague or inaccurate. In constrast, by asking questions that lead the respondent through nonthreatening items lending themselves to easy responses, the respondent becomes less threatened by the more sensitive questions. Following the latter design tends to increase truthfulness in responding and the number of questionnaires returned. As a matter of fact, the sequence noted above is appropriate for any instrument.

Question Placement

Place the easy, nonthreatening questions at the beginning of the questionnaire. These include traits such as: sex, job, age, marital status, number of children, whether the spouse works or not, and other nonthreatening demographic data. These items are not highly sensitive, although they are personal. In some cases questions about marital status or number of children may cause adverse reactions. You must evaluate that by knowing your population. As a category, these are usually classified as "demographic" questions. These informational questions are short, inoffensive, and allow the respondent to become accustomed to completing items. Once a responding behavior has been induced, the respondent is more committed to accomplishing the tasks and more sensitive questions are tolerated.

If a researcher desires to construct items which determine respondent consistency, they may be included in each section or topic. This usually requires that major opinion-seeking items be reworded in two or three different forms. In this manner the researcher can determine if the respondent is consistent when responding. (If there is little consistency, among questions, then the entire instrument may have dubious validity for that respondent.)

IN SUM

Stressed throughout this chapter is the point that good questionnaires are well planned and that each question or response item must be very carefully examined. The preplanning needed to construct a survey instrument pays off with valid data and a high response rate. In the next chapter the topic of preparing forced response questions will be addressed in great detail, with lesser attention to open-ended techniques.

CHAPTER 3

Designing Response Modes

Basically two response modes are used in questionnaire design: (1) forced-response and (2) open-ended. There are adaptations of these two formats, but forced-response formats are the most widely used. Each type is examined in this chapter.

MODES OF RESPONSE

Forced-Response Categories

Forced-response questions are designed to use response categories which are predetermined by the researcher. The categories of forced-response items require the respondent to mark one category only. This criterion requires the preparation of exhaustive (including all possible responses) and mutually exclusive items. The latter means that each response excludes all other possible responses, e.g., if a respondent is male--he cannot also be female.

In contrast, the items for forced-response categories which request the respondent to select all appropriate (more than one) categories must be exhaustive but not mutually exclusive. These items should provide alternatives for multiple responses, which are differentiated from each other.

Quite obviously, much study, advanced preparation, and anticipation of possible options must be accomplished by the investigator. Here is where the "review of literature" and previous research pays large dividends. If you desire to make comparisons with previously conducted surveys, then it will be important to identify and use the items being compared.

When it is not feasible to list all possible responses, an "other--please specify" category should be added. Use of this category, however, should be limited, due to difficulty in tabulating and interpreting results. Examples of these two types of forced-response items follow.

<u>Exhaustive and mutually exclusive</u>. One illustration of a mutually exclusive category is listed below.

1. Every high school student should be taught a marketable skill.

    ____ Strongly Agree
    ____ Agree
    ____ Undecided
    ____ Disagree
    ____ Strongly Disagree

The respondent can logically select only one category, because the categories are mutually exclusive. Note also that an equal number of positive and negative responses are presented, and that the statement is simple and written with a positive denotation.

<u>Categories for multiple responses</u>. In some cases the investigator may construct a checklist to determine broad categories for, perhaps, future follow-up. One example follows.

2. Universities should provide general university requirements for all students in which of the following applied areas? Mark any number of choices.

    ( ) Business Administration
    ( ) Communications--Oral
    ( ) Communications--Written

( ) Computer Programming
( ) Consumer Law
( ) Consumer Mathematics
( ) Rights under the Constitution
( ) Other--please specify_____

It would be impossible to list all of the applied skills that people may think should be taught in universities, therefore the "Other" category is provided. Respondents have a choice of marking any number of responses. The teaching of one applied skill does not exclude the teaching of others. Of course, if such a topic were to be surveyed, then there would be several generic clusters, and probably rank ordering of items.

Open-ended questions. An open-ended question does not typically include response categories. The respondent is free to respond in any desired manner. There are at least five reasons for using an open-ended question: (1) to probe an idea further, (2) to accommodate categories which are incomplete or inadequate in a forced-response list, (3) to provide projective types of situations, (4) to generate items for forced-response surveys, and (5) to elicit items for a Delphi technique (to be discussed in Chapter 6). Open-ended questions are inappropriate when forced-response categories can be formulated. Questions that can be answered yes or no or by degrees of agreement or disagreement should always be in a force-response format. Tabulating and quantifying results and researching meaningful generalizations are much easier with forced-response questions.

Open-ended questions require a more complex and usually subjective coding system than forced-response questions. Coding is explained in detail in Chapter 4. Be aware, however, that tabulating open-ended results requires examination of each respondent's answers on an individual basis. Categories for certain characteristics of the responses must be developed. Each of the open-ended responses is then classified into one of the appropriate groups. In contrast, the categories needed for forced-response questions are already developed for each respondent by virtue of the response pattern which is provided. Obviously, analyzing open-ended questions is more time consuming and subjective than analyzing forced-response questions. In some cases, the investigator may combine both types of questions. An example of a mixed open-ended question follows.

3. Do you feel every University student should be taught at least one marketable skill?
   ( ) Yes, please elaborate_____
   ( ) No, please elaborate_____

Another version of the same question as an open-ended question could be framed.

4. Recently, it has been written that every University student should be taught at least one marketable skill. What are your reactions to that statement?

   _____

It has been this writer's experience that when open-ended questions are used in some surveys, the rate of return tended to be rather low. In most cases, open-ended questionnaires require a greater amount of time to complete than does a forced-response one. Respondents, apparently, do not desire to devote the time needed to complete several items which may require lengthy responses, searching of files for information, or whatever. Open-ended surveys may obtain high responses if they are relevant to the respondents. The most critical problem, to repeat,

s to tabulate the information in a meaningful, systematic, and objective
anner. Open-ended questionnaires are valuable in generating initial lists,
ut probably that task should be accomplished with very small selected
roups. From the lists, forced-response items could then be generated.
n one sense, an open-response format connotes that the researcher has
ot explored the topic adequately and is simply "fishing" for responses.

There is yet another form of open-response--the volunteer remarks
ritten on forced-or open-response questionnaires by respondents who
pparently have strong feelings about the topic being investigated.
ith open-response items, the respondents who seem to be most concerned
end to write prolific statements. When an investigator begins to interpret
engthy monologues, it is usually difficult to quantify or, in some
ases, to even classify the comments.

Are comments helpful to the investigator? In at least one study
irected by the author (Orlich, Craven, and Rounds, 1968) it became apparent
hat the volunteer responses of the survey subjects tended not to
dd any substantial point to those which had been generated in the forced-
esponse instrument. An "n" of one is hardly conclusive, but the 1968
tudy was the third in a series directed by the author and the same
bservation was apparent in all three surveys.

Respondent comments in forced-response instruments must be carefully
nalyzed, lest a vociferous respondent bias the entire instrument. The
atter is all too obvious with student course evaluation questionnaires.
urther, comments should be quantified so that some trend may be observed
y the investigator. Long lists of respondent comments (or at worst,
arefully selected ones) taken from survey instruments can be misleading
nd possibly bias a reader's interpretation.

Convenience of form. Be certain that the respondent is able to reply in a manner that reflects precisely what is wanted. The entire questionnaire must be structured so that there will be little or no chance for confusion. Not only will respondents cooperate with instructions but a well-structured questionnaire lends itself to easy tabulation. Compare the first set of questions with the second set in the following examples.

Set 1. Circle your sex: Female___ Male___. Check your ethnic background, Black or Afro-American___ Oriental or Asian___ American Indian or other Native American___ Spanish Surname___ Caucasian (Other than Spanish surname)___ Other (please specify)___ Please write your year of birth____.

Set 2. Kindly check only one item for each question.

1. Your Sex is: (1) ___Female   (2) ___Male
2. Your ethnic background is:

    (1) ___Black or Afro-American
    (2) ___Oriental or Asian
    (3) ___American Indian or other Native American
    (4) ___Spanish surname
    (5) ___Caucasian (other than Spanish surname)
    (6) ___Other (please specify)_____

3. Your Age is:

    (1) ___19 or under
    (2) ___20-24
    (3) ___25-29
    (4) ___30-34
    (5) ___35-39
    (6) ___40 or over

The first set is awkward to follow and leads to respondent confusion. Further, the appearance gives the impression that not much effort or organization has been devoted to the instrument's preparation. The term instrument is used interchangeably with questionnaire.

The second set displays each question and response in a neat, organized fashion. Tabulation of the responses in the second example would also be accomplished much easier than for the first. In the Appendix there are displayed a series of models, question formats, and illustrations of how questions may be arranged for a wide variety of instrument styles. Since this section was concerned with mode, the next series of examples illustrates the construction of scales appropriate to forced-response items.

ESTABLISHING APPROPRIATE SCALES

Forced-response questions typically represent one of the three measurement scales (systems of numerical notation). It is important to distinguish among these scales when coding responses or conducting statistical analyses. A working knowledge of these scales will aid in designing more appropriate questions.

Nominal Scales

One common type of forced-response question represents the nominal or "naming" scale. The response categories of a nominal item are basically nonnumerical in their relationship. Nominal scales identify rather than measure. Questions representing a nominal scale are usually designed to gather factual (objective) information about the respondent. For example:

5. I am
    ____ (1) Male
    ____ (2) Female

Note that the response categories are both exhaustive and mutually exclusive when the respondent is required to mark only one category. The categories of the preceding example are exhaustive because the respondent must be either male or female, and the categories are mutually exclusive since the respondent cannot be a member of both.

In addition to factual information about the respondent, you may gather factual information, for example, about existing programs or school policies. All questions which require the respondent to answer "yes," "no," or "maybe" represent a nominal scale. For example:

6. Is a course about "Consumer Economics" now being taught in your high school?
   ____ (1) Yes
   ____ (2) No
   ____ (3) Do not know

As a note of interest, it must be observed that "Yes" or "No" responses are among the poorest forced-response categories to be used. In the example above, a response of "no" would be meaningful. It tells you that the school does not have such a course. But, if the respondent were to check "yes," you have virtually no information about the type of course, the typical enrollees, its content, or a host of other important descriptive items. If question 6 were used, then it would require several follow-up questions (within the instrument) for those who responded "yes" so that meaningful data could be obtained.

Ordinal Scales

The ordinal scale, which represents another type of forced-response question, is usually used to gather both factual information and respondent opinion. The ordinal scale indicates a rank order relationship among the response categories of a question; however, it does not reveal how much difference there is between the categories. For example:

7. Which of the following best compares your teaching load this year to your assigned teaching load for next year?

___(1) I will teach fewer classes next year.
___(2) I will teach the same number of classes next year.
___(3) I will teach a greater number of classes next year.

The response categories shown for question 7 have a definite mathematical relationship; "fewer" is less than "same" and both of these categories are less than "greater." However, the researcher cannot assume that there are equal differences between the categories "few" and "same," and the categories "same" and "greater." One respondent may be assigned to two fewer classes for next year, whereas another respondent may be assigned to one additional class for next year. Because the categories do not request the information, how many "fewer" or how many "greater" classes, equal distances cannot be assumed; nor can the class loads be determined in terms of student equivalents. If the latter is needed then a supplementary open-ended item might be used to determine the actual numbers.

Another method of gathering opinions on a systematic basis requires that respondents rank the categories of a question according to theie preference. Rank order questions also represent an _ordinal_ scale. For example, a respondent's general preference may reflect weak opinions that are rather difficult to differentiate. Consequently, there can be a greater difference in preference between the first and the second ranked items than there is between some generally noted preferences.

The researcher cannot determine the exact amount of differences between categories, but unequal differences are assumed when using ordinal systems. The following example illustrates a rank order question which seeks to obtain factual information:

8. The Department of Education is planning to publish a journal in the immediate future. Funds to support this endeavor have been made available from the "XYZ Foundation." We need your help to determine the types of topics you desire in the publication. Please rank order the following topics from one to six. Place a "1" in front of your first choice, "2" in from of your second choice, up to number "6" for your last choice. Please rank all categories, using each choice only once.

    _____ Administratively oriented articles
    _____ Curriculum and instruction topics
    _____ Evaluation designs
    _____ General articles about education and the field in overview.
    _____ Research findings applicable to the schools
    _____ School information, highlights, or critiques
    _____ Other (please specify) _____

The categories of a ranked item do not possess a mathematical relationship, per se. However, when the respondent ranks the categories, a mathematical and hierarchical relationship is established. If the above item were actually used, it would be most important to address other reader interest factors since the topics listed above are very general.

   Likert scales. The most widely used ordinal scale among survey researchers is called the Likert scale, named after its originator, Rensis Likert. Questions which require some form of rating usually represent Likert scales. Such scales, used primarily for assessing opinions, are usually composed of five or more response categories, e.g., Strongly agree, Agree, Undecided, Disagree, and Strongly disagree, or a similar continuum. The following examples represent Likert-type scale items.

9. More writing courses are needed in higher education.

   ( ) Strongly agree
   ( ) Agree
   ( ) Undecided
   ( ) Disagree
   ( ) Strongly disagree

10. I would encourage the school board to promote programs aimed at providing job skills to the physically and mentally handicapped.

    ( ) Encourage very much
    ( ) Encourage
    ( ) No Opinion
    ( ) Discourage
    ( ) Discourage very much

11. Rate yourself as a research design specialist:

    ( ) Excellent
    ( ) Good
    ( ) Undecided
    ( ) Poor
    ( ) Unsatisfactory

12. How well do you like attending workshops as compared to other instructional procedures?

    ( ) I like workshops much better.
    ( ) I like workshops a little better.
    ( ) I like all instructional procedures about equally well.
    ( ) I like other instructional procedures a little better than workshops.
    ( ) I like other instructional procedures much better than workshops.

13. In my high school, students call their teachers by their first names.

    ( ) Almost always
    ( ) Frequently
    ( ) Approximately equal in occurrence and nonoccurrence
    ( ) Infrequently
    ( ) Almost never

14. Would you tend to favor a new income tax as a way of reducing property taxes?

    ( ) Strongly favor
    ( ) Tend to favor
    ( ) Neither favor, nor oppose
    ( ) Tend to oppose
    ( ) Strongly oppose

15. Do you feel that as a classroom teacher you can now effectively use the tests which were covered in the workshop?

    ( ) Definitely yes
    ( ) Probably yes
    ( ) Uncertain
    ( ) Probably not
    ( ) Definitely not

16. I feel that extracurricular activities in high school are:

    ( ) Very important
    ( ) Important
    ( ) Undecided
    ( ) Unimportant
    ( ) Very unimportant

The respondent is requested to select only one category of a Likert scale item. The categories must be exhaustive and mutually exclusive. The above models and all others in this book are provided for your use. Please feel free to adapt them as you prepare items for surveys which you will conduct.

Since Likert Scales are most frequently used in questionnaire design, a somewhat comprehensive list of possible continua are provided in Model 3-1, to make your next set of choices a bit easier.

You will observe in the sixteen different continua shown in Model 3-1, that there are always two items that are positive, while there are always two that are negative. In many cases there is a neutral or "no opinion" position. The decision to use a neutral position depends on the investigator's desires. In some cases, you may desire a clear dichotomous

Model 3-1. A Sample of Likert Responses

Very adequate
Adequate
Inadequate
Very inadequate

Strongly agree
Agree
Undecided
Disagree
Strongly disagree

Strongly agree
Agree with reservations
No opinion
Disagree with reservations
Strongly disagree

Very clear
Somewhat clear
Somewhat unclear
Very unclear

Very conscientiously
Somewhat conscientiously
Somewhat unconscientiously
Very unconscientiously

Greatly encourage
Encourage
No opinion
Discourage
Greatly discourage

Strongly encourage
Encourage
No opinion
Discourage
Strongly discourage

Strongly favor
Tend to favor
No opinion
Tend to disfavor
Strongly disfavor

Very good
Good
No opinion
Poor
Very poor

Very important
Somewhat important
Undecided
Somewhat unimportant
Very unimportant

Very satisfactory
Satisfactory
Undecided
Unsatisfactory
Very unsatisfactory

Almost always supports
Usually supports
Usually unsupportive
Almost always unsupportive

Very supportive
Supportive
Unsupportive
Very unsupportive

Very good quality
Good quality
Uncertain
Poor quality
Very poor quality

Almost always valid
Usually valid
Usually invalid
Almost always invalid

Definitely yes
Probably yes
Uncertain
Probably no
Definitely no

---

distinction to be made by the respondent. In those cases, there will be no neutral position. The neutral position tends to allow the respondent an option "not to respond" for some reason. Further, a neutral item allows the investigator to determine the relative strength of some questions or issues. If many of the respondents express neither a positive nor negative feeling, then it may be assumed that the item is not a major concern of the group--if that is the case--or that the group does not have adequate information to take a position.

Interval Scales

The most sophisticated scale used by survey researchers is the interval scale. The term "interval" connotes a rank order relationship with equal differences between categories. The latter characteristic distinguishes the interval from the ordinal scale. The following question uses the interval scale.

17. How many secondary school students attended your high school (grades 9-12 or 10-12) for 1977-78?

    _____ (1) 1,000 or more
    _____ (2) 750-999
    _____ (3) 500-749
    _____ (4) 250-499
    _____ (5) 249 or less

Four of the above categories have a 250 point interval, making these categories equidistant. The category of "1,000 or more" may not be assumed to be equidistant. Again, this illustrates the need of prior knowledge: in this instance, the upper limits of secondary schools. By using internal data and meeting the assumption relevant to parametric tests, more powerful or comprehensive statistical analyses may be used by the researchers. This point might be critical in selected studies.

A commonly used device in the construction of interval scales is to request relative judgments about the quality of people or products. Typical of such interval scales is the following example:

21. Where would you rank this individual among the group?

    ____ Upper 10%
    ____ Upper 25%
    ____ Upper 50%
    ____ Lower 50%
    ____ Lower 25%
    ____ Lower 10%

Another form of the above scale, but in which the intervals are unequal, yet consistent and proportional, is:

22. How would you judge the performance of this individual with others who do similar tasks?

    ____ Upper 10%
    ____ Upper 25%
    ____ Middle 50%
    ____ Lower 25%
    ____ Lower 10%

Although the distances between specific items are unequal there is a connotation of equal spacing within the spectrum units.

Transforming Items

Nominal, ordinal, and interval data may require different coding techniques and forms of statistical analysis. Therefore, it is important to know precisely which scale a forced-response question represents. It is an acceptable procedure to regroup data by converting from a higher to a lower order of measurement (from interval to ranked to nominal). But, conversion from a lower to a higher order is not logically accomplished. For example, consider age data and how they can be described using nominal, ordinal, and interval scales.

Interval scale: 18. Your age group is:

    ____(1) 19 or under
    ____(2) 20-24
    ____(3) 25-29
    ____(4) 30-34
    ____(5) 35-39
    ____(6) 40-44
    ____(7) 45-49
    ____(8) 50-54
    ____(9) 55-59
    ____(10) 60 or over

Ordinal scale: 19. Your age group is:

    ____(1) Adolescent
    ____(2) Adult
    ____(3) Middle age
    ____(4) Retirement age

Nominal scale: 20. Were you born during the baby boom, i.e., between 1946 and 1950?

    ____(1) Yes
    ____(2) No

In these illustrations, the interval scale includes the information sought in both the ordinal and nominal forms. By using the interval form, more precise information can be obtained, plus the option of regrouping the data into more general categories. To change the item from interval to ordinal data, one could assign the "19 or under" category to the adolescent group; categories "20-24," "25-29," "30-34," and "35-39" to the adult group; categories "40-44," "45-49," and "50-54" to the middle age group; and the "60 and over" to the retirement age group. Similarly, to change the item from an interval to a nominal item, one could assign category "25-29" to the "yes" group, and all other categories to the "no" group. The reverse procedure, changing nominal to interval data, cannot be accomplished because the nominal response categories are less specific and thus less informative than the interval categories.

The interval scale of ages in five-year brackets is a most useful one, since it is the same interval used by the U.S. Bureau of the Census. By using their divisions, comparisons are easily made between any self-made item and those nationally collected. Traits such as age, income, level of schooling, occupational group, and several others should always be standardized with Bureau of the Census categories. Meaningful, critical, or statistical analyses may then be made on validly collected data for regional, national, or occupational surveys.

Other Considerations

If forced-response items are used, then an investigator must adequately anticipate all the significant alternatives without overlap. Further, all items must be logically or consistently ordered and the wording of items must be impartial and unbiased. Designing forced-response categories that obtain accurate results requires careful consideration for every alternative. Often questionnaires contain alternatives which are too similar, thus unnecessarily dividing responses.

The following continuum, or one very similar to it, is often used to determine the use of some teaching method or the availability of an educational product. The question is typically stated as:

23. How many times do you use the overhead projector in your classes?

```
23.1 _____ always
23.2 _____ usually
23.3 _____ sometimes
23.4 _____ infrequently
23.5 _____ seldom
23.6 _____ never
```

Other than always and never, the spectrum of responses is so very close that it is almost impossible to draw worthwhile or reliable conclusions.

One better method is to place some precise or quantitative elements in the continuum. In the case cited above, at least a more definitive set of conclusions could be inferred if the response set were:

```
24.1 _____ every day
24.2 _____ at least once a week
24.3 _____ at least once a month
24.4 _____ at least once every two months
24.5 _____ never
24.6 _____ other (please specify)
```

Other biases may be incorporated into a survey instrument if the investigator does not analyze each set of responses for equal weighting, or in controversial issues, positive, neutral, and negative positions.

For example, assume that a survey of public opinion concerning the effectiveness of reading in elementary schools is planned. If a disproportionate number of questions are concerned with the positive aspects of the curriculum, possible negative public attitudes may not be elicited. The item which follows illustrates this bias.

25. Concerning our elementary reading program, to what extent do you think it is doing a good job in teaching the children to read?

```
( )  25.1  Doing great
( )  25.2  Doing an adequate job
( )  25.3  Doing about as good a job as we can afford
( )  25.4  Could be improved
( )  25.5  Not doing a good job
```

Note above that four of the five responses are positively oriented, while only one is clearly negative. There is no neutral response. On any random sample the bias ought to show 80 percent responding favorable to this item and 20 percent responding negatively. The above bias is frequently observed.

To alleviate either positive or negative bias, as may be the case, a response set of five should contain the following elements:

( ) 1. Very positive response
( ) 2. Positive response
( ) 3. Neutral response
( ) 4. Negative response
( ) 5. Very negative response

The model above is mandatory for Likert-type response sets.

If a researcher desires to use but three items in a response set, then a positive, neutral, and negative spectrum should be used. Biases can be built into forced-response items--either by purposeful design or ignorance. It is recognized that a portion of this section is repetitive from Chapter 2. However, the points are critical, and thus need additional emphasis.

The designs for response modes may be easily integrated into your total survey purposes and objectives. Surveys may have a variety of responses modes if the information being elicited lends itself to multiple modality. After designing the items and response modes you must address the problem of coding the items: The topic presented in Chapter 4.

CHAPTER 4

Coding Survey Items

FORCED-RESPONSE CODES

Data obtained from interviews and questionnaires are not necessarily usable in the exact form in which they are collected. Raw data are usually converted to some quantitative form for analysis and display. The converting process is called scoring or coding. Most forced-response questions can be precoded prior to questionnaire distribution with ease. The researcher simply assigns, in advance, a numerical score to each response category. Then each response can be immediately and directly converted into a score (quantified) in an objective, consistent, and systematic manner.

<u>Coding nominal data</u>. The response categories of a nominal question do not have quantitative relationships to each other. Therefore, numerical symbols for coding are assigned by using a systematic method. Consider the following example:

1. I plan on seeking a full time job in my hometown after university graduation.

    _____ (1) Yes
    _____ (2) Undecided
    _____ (3) No

Assigned is a code of (1) to the response "yes," a code of (3) to the response "no," and a code of (2) to the response "undecided." This coding system does not imply that the response "yes" (code 1) is less than the response "no" (code 3). The numerical codes for nominal data imply identify mutually exclusive categories. Nominal data items can then be analyzed by a simple count of the number of respondents who marked category 1, the number who marked category 2, and the number who marked category 3. The above coding system is useful for all questions of similar construction in the questionnaire. In that manner a uniform coding system is maintained. Later in this chapter, there will be illustrated how the coding process may be transformed to electronic data processing cards.

Coding ordinal and interval items. The response categories of ordinal and interval items do have a quantitative relationship, therefore numerical symbols should be assigned consistently. Consider the following example:

2. Which of the following best compares this year's (1977-78) engineering curriculum to next year's (1978-79) engineering curriculum?

    _____ (1) Fewer classes will be offered next year
    _____ (2) Same for both years
    _____ (3) More classes will be offered next year

For this example, "fewer classes" (code 1) is less than "same" (code 2) and code 1 and code 2 are both less than "more classes" (code 3). Ordinal and interval data of these types can be analyzed by counting the number of respondents who marked each category. Note, in the example, that the date is included in the question to aid in precise and explicit interpretation.

Ranked items are scored individually by each respondent, who is requested to number a set of categories according to some criterion. Consider the following example:

3. Did you attend University Day because: (Please rank the following five items according to your reasons for attending. Place a "1" in front of the primary reason, a "2" in front of the second most important reason, and so on until you have ranked all five items. You may use a ranking number only once.)

    1. ____ Parents suggested attendance
    2. ____ High school counselor suggested attendance
    3. ____ Saw advertisement on local TV which influenced you
    4. ____ Friends suggested attendance
    5. ____ Saw or heard about it in high school
    6. ____ Other (please specify) _____

Each ranked category requires one response, and can be viewed as a separate question. In the above example, each respondent ranks every category. Ranked items can be analyzed by determining the mean rank score for each response category.

<u>Coding Likert scale items</u>. The Likert scale is most frequently used to obtain ordinal data. The instrument is designed so that a respondent selects one of five categories that best describes an opinion toward the question. The response categories of a Likert scale item <u>do have</u> a quantitative relationship and consecutive scores must be assigned to consecutive categories. For example:

4. My children are receiving adequate vocational counseling in high school.

    ( ) Strongly agree ( ) Agree ( ) No opinion ( ) Disagree ( ) Strongly disagree

Usually you will assign a code of "five" to Strongly agree, a code of "four" to Agree, a code of "three" to No opinion, a code of "two" to

Disagree, and a code of "one" to Strongly disagree. The order must be followed consistently throughout your instrument. Typically the highest number is assigned to the most positive response and the lowest number to the most negative response.

Coding subscales of Likert scale items. Often a questionnaire will contain a number of subscales, each of which measures a different aspect of the total scale. For example, if the purpose of the survey is to measure the community need for a specific aspect of a general education program, part of the questionnaire may ask four or five questions pertaining to the respondent's attitude toward general education in the comprehensive high school. These four or five questions comprise a subscale, and are viewed as a group because each question attempts to discover the same attitude from a different perspective. When you rely on more than one question to assess an attitude, the response reliability is greater. Questions composing a subscale should be distributed throughout the questionnaire so that a respondent must consider each question individually rather than simply falling into a "response pattern syndrome" or "mind set." However, you may decide to group all subscales into separate sections of the questionnaire for ease of administration and analysis.

A few of the questions composing a subscale should be worded such that if the respondent agrees with a statement, e.g., the present general education courses, there will be a positive response. Other questions in the same subscale, however, should be so worded such that the respondent who is not pleased with the present general education courses will respond negatively. Reverse wording alleviates biasing a subscale and provides a means by which to ascertain respondent consistency. For example, the following pair of questions are reversely worded.

5. Students enrolled in general education courses in high school tend to be adequately trained.

( ) Strongly ( ) Agree ( ) Undecided ( ) Disagree ( ) Strongly
    agree   disagree

. . . .

6. Students who receive general education training in the high school tend to be inadequately trained.

( ) Strongly ( ) Agree ( ) Undecided ( ) Disagree ( ) Strongly
    agree   disagree

A respondent who strongly favors the general education program will mark "Strongly agree" to the first question and "Strongly disagree" to the second question. These questions are called reversed items. One problem, however, of using negatively denoted statements is that such wording tends to bias the respondent to react in a rather atypical manner.

The purpose of using and analyzing a subscale is to assess the overall opinion toward an issue. Affirmative responses toward the issue must be coded in one direction while all negative responses toward the issue must be coded in the opposite direction. In Table 4-1 is an illustration of the coding procedure for reverse items.

Table 4-1. Scoring of Reversed Questions

	Scale Scores				
Affirmative Response (Question 5)	Most Positive			Most Negative	
	5	4	3	2	1
Continuum	Strongly agree	Agree	Undecided	Disagree	Strongly disagree
	Most Negative			Most Positive	
Negative Response (Question 6)	1	2	3	4	5

In this example, code 5 in questions 5 and 6 refers to a positive response toward the issue, while code 1 in questions 5 and 6 refers to a negative response to the issue. The respondent who highly favors the affirmative responses will receive a score of 10, while the respondent who highly disfavors the proposal will receive a score of 2. If the coding were not reversed for these two questions, the respondent who highly favors the program would receive the same score as the respondent who highly disfavors the program. To evaluate the group of questions as a subscale, you must code according to the response toward the issue that the subscale as a whole is attempting to assess. Observe the coding possibilities of the following items. The responses are listed below.

7. I enjoy myself most of the time in school.
    ( ) Strongly ( ) Agree ( ) Undecided ( ) Disagree ( ) Strongly
        agree   disagree
8. When I am in school I usually feel unhappy.
    ( ) Strongly ( ) Agree ( ) Undecided ( ) Disagree ( ) Strongly
        agree   disagree

Table 4-2. Two Alternative Coding Systems

	Scale Scores				
(Question 7) enjoy	1	2	3	4	5
Continuum	Strongly agree	Agree	Undecided	Disagree	Strongly disagree
(Question 8) unhappy	5	4	3	2	1
	Scale Scores				
(Question 7) enjoy	5	4	3	2	1
Continuum	Strongly agree	Agree	Undecided	Disagree	Strongly disagree
(Question 8) unhappy	1	2	3	4	5

Observe that the codes are displayed in two distinct forms, but always in a consistent manner. Caution must always be exercised when establishing coding criteria so that the same directionality is maintained for a study. You should maintain a definite scaling order, with the most positive being always "5," while the most negative is always "1" (on a five point continuum), to be most logical. By analyzing the scores you can identify trends by question score patterns.

There is yet another technique that you can use to avoid having the respondents become rather "automatic" in their responses. The technique is simply to change the order of the response codes so that they reflect a somewhat random sequencing. Observe the example below in which the typical 5 point Likert response scale consists of: 5 for Strongly agree, 4 for Agree, 3 for No opinion, 2 for Disagree, and 1 for Strongly disagree. The statements would be represented by the row of x's. Note how a random rotation of the number patterns causes the respondent to think about each response--there is no simple rushing through the list: You must carefully locate each coded response item.

Statements	Code to be Circled
1. xxxxxxxxxxxxxxxxxxxxxxxxx	5 4 3 2 1
2. xxxxxxxxxxxxxxxxxxx	3 5 1 2 4
3. xxxxxxxxxxxxxxxxxxxxxxx	2 5 4 1 3
4. xxxxxxxxxxxxxxxxxxxxx	4 3 2 5 1

The above system eliminates the use of confusing "negative" items. This response technique could also replace the use of reverse-scored questions and thus reduce the chances for a respondent's loss of patience. The method is also coded for electronic data processing, since the numerical codes are not changed. If you have any suspicion that the respondents might be either "yes" or "no" oriented or are not carefully considering the responses, then the adaptation of this method would alleviate the problem. Coding forced-response items is rather simple. But, what of open-ended items?

OPEN RESPONSE CODES

<u>Coding open-ended items.</u> Open-ended items usually need to be quantified so that an analysis or summary of the questionnaire may be more objectively derived. Coding an open-ended question involves superimposing some type of structured format to the free or unstructured responses. For efficiency, researchers often establish precoded response categories in anticipation of responses to open-ended questions. The extent to which precoding is possible is an indication of the extent to which the question is likely to yield relevant information. To avoid coding unreliably, open-ended responses should be coded independently by at least two judges. It is the responsibility of the judges to categorize the unstructured responses according to the predetermined coding system. The coders must be trained in advance by the researcher.

The following question is an open-ended item:

9. At what grade levels do you think children should be taught about careers and the world of work as a part of the school program?

The respondent is free to express an opinion in any manner. One respondent may write a paragraph describing the background information that led to the decision, another may write one word describing the opinion. Regardless of the length, some systematic method of interpreting the responses must be addressed early in the planning stages.

To establish precoded categories for an item, a researcher must know why the question is being asked and anticipate types of responses. The following are at least two possible coding systems for the above item:

```
____ Grades 1-3              ____ Elementary school
____ Grades 4-6              ____ Junior high school
____ Grades 7-8     (or)     ____ Senior high school
____ Grades 9-10             ____ Post secondary school
____ Grades 11-12
```

Why is coding essential for open-ended questions? At the outset, this question may seem to be ridiculous. But, if you ask questions in which massive amounts of information are returned but cannot be categorized--that is all that you have--massive amounts of information. Surveys have a focus. Open-ended questions tend to act like those hideous "Party Line" telephone programs conducted by hundreds of radio stations. Generalizations are difficult to draw from open questions that have been loosely responded to. How does one, for example, draw inferences from paragraphs of rambling prose? The latter seems to typify the answers to open-ended questionnaires.

The elaboration about open-ended responses is to stress their difficulty in reporting results in an objective and accurate manner. Typically such items lead to inconclusive generalizations and highly subjective interpretations. Focus is structured by the questionnaire developer. The sharper the focus and responses, the more conclusive the generalizations.

<u>Coding checklist items.</u> Checklist items are a reasonable alternative to open-ended items because they give the respondent some latitude, and also provide preidentified categories which are usable for coding. A checklist question is a special form of a forced-response item which allows for multiple responses. For example:

10. Children should be taught about careers and the world of work as a part of the school program at which grade level(s). (Check as many as you desire.)

        10.1 ____ Grades 1-3
        10.2 ____ Grades 4-6
        10.3 ____ Grades 7-8
        10.4 ____ Grades 9-10
        10.5 ____ Grades 11-12

To code multiple response items, each category must be viewed as a separate question to which the respondents answer might be classed as "agree" or "disagree." The respondent has the option to mark as many or as few categories as is desired. The categories are not mutually exclusive and therefore the respondent considers each category independently. Within each category, a negative response, "disagree" or "no," may be coded "1", while the opposite response may be coded "2." Maintain the selected coding system for the entire study to assure uniform reporting.

    Occasionally, checklist items will include a category titled "Other, please specify." If the researcher is interested in analyzing these responses, the category must be approached like an open-ended item. Responses must be assigned to subcategories and each subcategory must be analyzed individually.

    Checklists do cause problems of interpretation. Other than respondent counting, little analysis can be accomplished. In many cases, checklists could be converted to more informative modes.

    For example, checklists may also be constructed to use a modified Likert scale concomitantly. Observe in Model 4-1 below how question 10, previously cited, can be constructed to use Likert designs.

Model 4-1. Combining Checklist and Likert Designs

10A. Kindly respond to each item by circling one of the numbers which represents your attitude to each part of the question. The coded numbers mean:

>   5 = Strongly agree
>   4 = Agree
>   3 = No opinion
>   2 = Disagree
>   1 = Strongly disagree

11-16. To what extent do you agree that children at each specified grade level should be taught about careers and the world of work as a part of the school program? Please respond to each grade level.

		Strongly agree	Agree	No opinion	Disagree	Strongly disagree
11.	Grades 1-3	5	4	3	2	1
12.	Grades 4-6	5	4	3	2	1
13.	Grades 7-8	5	4	3	2	1
14.	Grades 9-10	5	4	3	2	1
15.	Grades 11-12	5	4	3	2	1
16.	Post secondary schools	5	4	3	2	1

Note how construction of the series shown in 10A, 11-16, provides more specific data to the researcher. Although a basic checklist has been used, each item is judged on an absolute scale; whereas in checklist format no discrimination is made between items. Every "check" is of equal weight. By combining checklist format with Likert design the focus of the question gains both a quantitative dimension and a qualitative one. Nearly all checklists and rank order tests can be adapted to a mixed design.

Coding is a necessary procedure for analyzing and displaying survey data. A working knowledge of the types of forced-response questions aids in developing a consistent and accurate coding system. Preplanning will not only make the coding procedure more efficient, but will improve the accuracy of the instrument.

Another aspect of preplanning is to consider the coding for data processing. In most surveys, some type of electronic data processing (EDP) will be used. The cost, time, and handling factors are now such that even the most simply designed survey--or the most complicated one--is most effectively tabulated and displayed via EDP. Let us briefly review those planning considerations.

ELECTRONIC DATA PROCESSING

Data are easily tabulated and analyzed by electronic processing equipment. Used in the process are three or four standard pieces of machinery: key punch, card sorter, electronic computer, and printer. These items of equipment are accessible in most towns. Most vocational schools, community colleges, state colleges, and universities invariably possess the equipment, and are easily accessable to process outside data, usually charging nominal fees, usually for personnel costs. Private business charge slightly higher fees for the same service.

Tabulation of data and analytic requirements for the questionnaire should be planned in accordance with a potential budget *before* the survey begins. If electronic data processing is planned, the instrument should be examined by a data processing specialist <u>before the questionnaire is printed.</u> It is very sad for new researchers to determine, after data have been collected, that the items are not transferable to data cards. Protect your study by seeking expert advice in the very early planning stages.

Coding

Data are transferred from each questionnaire to an electronic data processing (EDP) card, which is a medium for systematic representation. The illustrated EDP card (Figure 4-2), also called an "IBM card," is divided into 80 vertical columns, with 10 numbered spaces in each vertical column, zero through nine. Data are made machine readable by assigning one or more specified vertical columns of the card to coincide with a designated questionnaire item. Spaces are assigned within that column to each of the various possible response categories. It is most efficient when transferring the data to the card if the questionnaire item number is coded to correspond directly to the vertical column number of the EDP card.

For example, if the first item of a questionnaire requests the respondent age and there are fewer than 10 response possiblities, that item can be represented in one vertical column. If the age data are subdivided into 5 categories, 6 of the 10 numbered spaces of the column will be needed to represent the respondents' ages. Row 0 is usually reserved to indicate "no response" to the question. The response category coded as "1" should be represented in <u>row 1</u> for easy transfer of data. By numbering the specific response categories to coincide with the row numbers, a simple

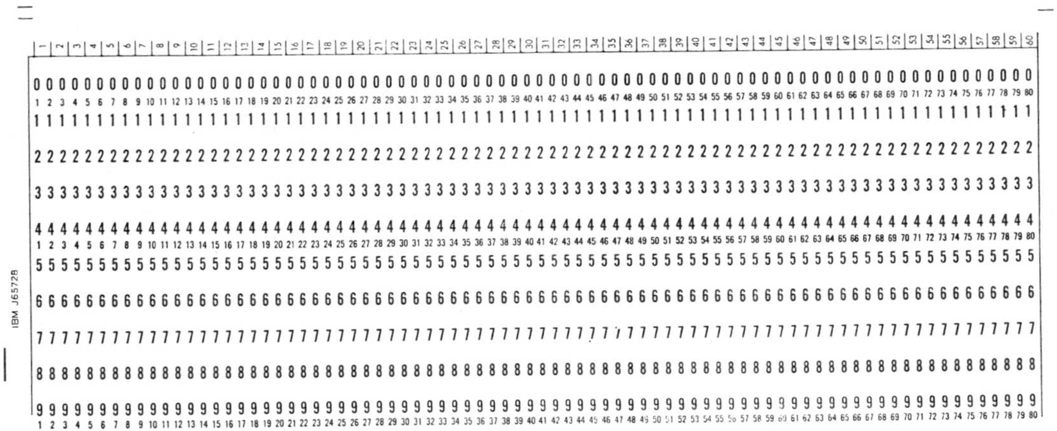

Figure 4-2. Typical Electronic Data Processing Card

coding device is automatically established by your questionnaire. See the Appendix, Model A-1 to observe a built-in transfer feature to EDP.

A single EDP card normally accommodates one respondent. If more than 80 vertical columns are needed to record the responses of one individual two or more cards are necessary. The last few vertical columns should be used to mark the card for identification. As a check against transfer errors, each respondent should be assigned an identification number to be written on both the original questionnaire and punched into the appropriate EDP card. The identification number should be posted with the respondent list, also, as a means to follow-up the nonrespondents. If more than one card per respondent is necessary, the card number (1, 2, 3, etc.) should be indicated on the EDP card in a specified column.

Precoding

Precoding a questionnaire allows one to key punch and machine tabulate directly from the questionnaire. Precoding forced-response data involves assigning questionnaire items and response categories to EDP card columns and rows <u>in advance</u> of printing the final questionnaire. Notations can be made on the questionnaire which indicate the assigned EDP codes. There are two steps involved in precoding a questionnaire: The first is the careful assigning of questions to the card columns, the second is the matching of the item responses to the rows.

<u>Column assignments</u>. Card and column assignments should be indicated for each question. Typically, the column number is shown in parentheses in the left margin beside each item. This should be done inconspicuously so as not to distract the respondent. Otherwise, explain the use of these

numbers to the respondent in the introduction or cover letter. The illustration below shows a precoded questionnaire item.

    17. Which of the following best compares this year's (1977-78) teacher education curriculum to next year's (1978-79) planned teacher education curriculum?

        _____ (1) Fewer classes will be offered next year
        _____ (2) Same for both years
        _____ (3) More classes will be offered next year

In this example, column 17 of the EDP card will be used to represent and correspond to question 17. It is more expedient when the questionnaire item number and the column number are the same, but this is not always possible with ranked or checklist items.

Another format may be used for the same question: The question and responses remain the same, but the response items have a numerical system that identifies both the column and the row. For example:

    17. Which of the following best compares this year's (1977-78) teacher education curriculum to next year's (1978-79) planned teacher education curriculum?

        17.1 _____ Fewer classes will be offered next year
        17.2 _____ Same for both years
        17.3 _____ More classes will be offered next year

The numbers could follow the blank, as below:

        _____ 17.1 Fewer classes will be offered next year
        _____ 17.2 Same for both years
        _____ 17.3 More classes will be offered next year

The examples above show that column 17 will use three rows: one, two, and three. Again, nonresponses to the question would automatically be marked in row zero. (Nonresponses, plus all responses, must be totaled.)

Either system is efficient, saves valuable time in transferring data, and reduces key punch errors.

Row codes. The second task in precoding involves row assignments within a given column. If there are nine or fewer response categories to an item, assign the categories to rows 1-9. Reserve row "zero" to represent "no response." Only one space in each column may be punched. In the case of ranked and checklist items, where the respondent is required to respond to more than one category, each category must be represented by a separate column on the data card. The assigned ranking by respondents for a particular response category should be punched in the row which corresponds to the ranked number and in the column which represents that response category. Rank ordered or checklist items require more columns on the EDP card than do nominal, ordinal, or interval items whose categories are mutually exclusive.

In the event that the responses require multiple columns or rows, then the coding and numbering system must accommodate the situation. For example, if you desire to code each of the 50 United States by numbers 1 to 50, then you would reserve two columns for this item. More than likely the states would be numbered in alphabetical order. If columns 16 and 17 were reserved for this item then 0 1 (punched in columns 16 and 17 respectively) would represent the first state. The code 5 0 would represent the fiftieth. For ease of coding you might even number that question as:

    16-17.   In which state do you now reside?

                       ___ ___ (Please place the state code number in the spaces to the left.)

By using the above technique, your respondents accomplish both the response and the code. You must, of course, provide an attached list of states and their respective code numbers, and any other code numbers that would be needed by the respondents.

Keep a code book or log which describes all questionnaire items and response categories and their locations on EDP cards. In simple surveys, it is sufficient to list these assignments on a blank copy of the questionnaire. More elaborate designs may require a code sheet specifically designed for the survey, or a manual system by which to assign code numbers. Several models are illustrated in the Appendix which show how instruments may be easily adapted for EDP coding.

If a precoded questionnaire contains proper indications of columns and row punch assignments, direct keypunching from the questionnaire to the EDP card is possible. To accomplish this, all questionnaires should be first edited to clarify or assign "zeros" to any ambiguous responses. Those questions that are unanswered or are incorrectly completed should be automatically assigned a zero. <u>Never</u> "correct" or "modify" a statement--that is called "altering the data."

The layout of a questionnaire is extremely important to aid direct key punching. Question items and response categories should be located in distinct patterns for ease of reading and transferring of responses to EDP cards.

When the response categories of some items cannot be precoded, it is necessary to prepare data transfer sheets for keypunching. Five different sets of data transfer sheets are illustrated in Table 4-3.

Table 4-3. Representative Data Response Models*

Blocked Column- Question Items	Open Numbered System	Closed Precoded System	Open Precoded System	Parentheses Precoded System
(1)	1.			
	___ (1)	1.1 ___	___ 1.1	( ) 1.1
	___ (2)	1.2 ___	___ 1.2	( ) 1.2
	___ (3)	1.3 ___	___ 1.3	( ) 1.3
(2)	2.			
	___ (1)	2.1 ___	___ 2.1	( ) 2.1
	___ (2)	2.2 ___	___ 2.2	( ) 2.2
	___ (3)	2.3 ___	___ 2.3	( ) 2.3

*Only one of the five modes would be used throughout. It is not advisable to mix modes.

Each respondent is represented by a separate data sheet. All responses are manually transferred to the code sheet. In some cases, the actual coding or transferring to the code sheet may be accomplished by the respondent. In the latter case, the respondent is provided with the survey instrument and a response code sheet. The instructions to the respondents must be most explicit so that all responses are made on the code sheet in a prescribed manner. This method reduces the costs of mailing, for only the response sheet is returned, while the respondent keeps the instrument.

The key puncher simply transfers the data from the code sheet to an EDP card. (If possible, optical scan equipment might even be used.) The code sheet must be totally consistent with the EDP card so that no "guesses" have to be made by the keypuncher. Any irregularities should be coded as "zero" by the coder or the investigator, not by the keypunch operator. Keypunchers do not like to make decisions--it slows their work and in most cases they do not know anything about the study, per se.

Subdividing into groups. A punched deck of EDP cards is ready for virtually any type of analysis. The deck can be fed through a card sorter, which simply counts the number of respondents who marked each category. The card sorter can also be used to separate cards according to specified categories, and then to subdivide the categories according to any selected item. For example, the cards may be separated according to sex. In this case, there would be two decks: one representing males and the other representing females. The researcher may then want to subdivide according to age. Each deck would be fed into the card sorter, so that all males and all females would be divided according to age categories. See Figure 4-3.

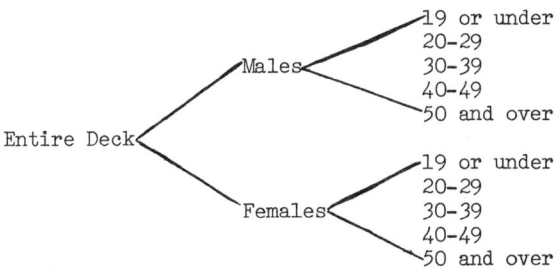

Figure 4-3. Subdivision of Two Questionnaire Items for Subgroup Analyses and Comparisons

The card sorter does the same type of analysis that can be done when using hand tabulations. With the card sorter (or computer), subsorts or sorts by categories can be accomplished for an unlimited set of arrays and all within a relatively few minutes. Such immediate output allows the researcher to spend more time interpreting the data, rather than simply tabulating it.

By planning for subgroup analyses, the investigator can easily compare the response patterns for specified groups. It is through this method that critical analyses are inferred. The testing of stated hypotheses are accomplished easily and with little effort by appropriate subgrouping. By using subgroup analytic techniques the investigator might also be able to compare results of one survey with those of other comparable ones. Your author cautiously adds that if you do not analyze your data by meaningful subgroups, you probably do not have a survey--you have a collection of numbers!

Punched EDP cards are "fed" into a computer which is accompanied by a program specifying the desired output or analysis. There are numerous preprinted programs (commonly called "canned programs") that usually require a few additional computer instruction cards. Programs can be selected that range from simple means and percentage calculations to complex statistical analyses.

The advantages of electronic data processing are numerous. The researcher's time is greatly economized by the speed with which electronic data are tabulated and printed into form for analysis. Accuracy is improved because humans are involved in fewer steps: There is less opportunity for human error. Also, a deck of EDP cards can be used again and again for different analyses by selecting different subsorts or programs. Although organizing the survey may take somewhat longer when using electronic data processing, the payoff to the investigator can be most substantial because detailed analyses of the data can be conducted. The EDP deck can be stored for future or long range comparisons.

In some cases, percentages are very adequate. In other situations, you will use inferential statistics. Whatever treatments are desired, the computer can be programmed to display the data in most nearly any form desired--including tables, charts, diagrams, histograms, pie graphs, line graphs, and even three dimensional renderings. These displays may be either copied or pasted-up for copying by any dry copy process. Again, this saves valuable time and money when preparing the final report.

All of these tasks require initial preplanning. Your writer's experience has demonstrated that more time is devoted to the planning of a survey than to any other phase or groups of tasks.

But, the survey must be conducted, so Chapter 5 addresses that topic.

CHAPTER 5

Conducting the Survey

Another major task in conducting any survey is to identify from the population a representative group who can provide the most representative information to help achieve the objectives of the survey. These selected persons are often called the "target population."

A target population may include more than just a single interest group. For example, a recent set of studies in Washington State wanted to assess attitudes about expanding vocational education sites outside of the existing high school facilities. School district policy makers determined that it would be important to obtain attitudes not only from the vocational and career instructional personnel of the school, but also from parents, students, patrons, business persons, and other groups. By incorporating these segments of the educational community, the investigators provided school district officials differing points of view on which to base decisions--decisions based on relevant, representative and meaningful data.

SAMPLING CONSIDERATIONS

Surveys conducted by educators or graduate students tend to involve a known, homogeneous group of people (finite population). For example, all the public high school principals in a state or all seniors of one high school might be the target population. The persons to be surveyed (sample of respondents) might include the entire target population, and the conclusions relate to the drawn sample only. In such cases, absolute conclusions cannot be made about the entire universe--all principals or all seniors. For example, if a survey of 100 seniors is conducted, the investigator cannot simply conclude that all seniors in high school follow the patterns of those sampled. However, one may cautiously apply the findings from the sample to the entire population--if the sample were representative of the universe.

Surveying the entire population of a comparatively small group eliminates the chance of sampling bias and is the preferred procedure. Improper sampling techniques (usually lack of representativeness) almost always lead to biased surveys. However, sampling techniques need not lead to biases if precautions are taken. When samples are drawn from any population, all members (the universe) of the population must have an equal chance of being selected. Simple random sampling or stratified random sampling are two basic recommended techniques. These sampling techniques will be discussed as will be that of disproportional sampling.

Random Techniques

Simple random sampling is effective if a listing of the total population is available. A telephone book is not a total listing of the total population because such a list usually discriminates against the poor and is inaccurate since a large number of persons change residences, leave town, or have unlisted numbers. Further, telephone directories usually list only the male head of the family, thereby causing a bias against women. City directories are also frequently neither current nor accurate. For example, your author drew a 1,000 person systematic-random sample from a telephone directory. Immediately after the questionnaires were mailed, over 150 were returned with the U.S. Postal Service stamp stating: "Moved--No Forwarding Address!" Typically, however, populations in school related surveys will be a more confined or homogeneous group, such as parents of high school students or home economics teachers in a specific region. Regardless of the size, the drawn sample must be representative of the target population.

Drawing. Once the target population is defined, one simple method of selecting a random sample is to assign a number to each member of the population. Corresponding numbers are then written on slips of paper with one slip representing each member of the population. The slips of paper are then placed in a container and thoroughly mixed. Slips of paper are then drawn individually to identify those who will comprise the sample.

Using random numbers. A table of random numbers or a computerized method may be more desirable and systematic for selecting random samples for larger surveys. These methods are also most appropriate for smaller surveys. Remember, when using simple random sampling, the entire population must be clearly defined and it must be equally possible for each member to be chosen for the sample.

Stratified Samples

Stratified sampling is a method used to obtain a greater degree of representation. Rather than being selected as a random sample from the total population, appropriate members are drawn from known homogeneous subsets of that population in the proportions in which they exhibit chosen traits. In a study of high school students, for example, the researcher may first organize the population by class and draw a predetermined number of freshmen, sophomores, juniors, and seniors. The drawing must representative of the percentage of the total for each "class" to be classified as "stratified."

A researcher might wish to utilize an even more complex stratification method. In addition to stratifying by class, the researcher might also stratify by sex, by grade point average (GPA), or other key traits. In this fashion, the sample can be selected to contain equivalent numbers of boys and girls, each exhibiting the desired GPA by class, age, or whatever.

The choice of stratification variables typically depends on those variables which are exhibited by the population and on the goal of the survey. In selecting stratification variables from among those available, the researcher should be concerned primarily that those selected are represented accurately. Demographic and geographic traits are frequently used to stratify populations.

The method of stratification usually requires grouping the population into discrete groups based on the selected stratification variables. On the basis of the relative proportion of the population represented by a given group, a number of elements from that group are selected--either randomly or systematically. For example, if one group resides in a specified geographic area and comprises 10 percent of the population, and a sample of 1,000 is desired, then 100 persons residing in that area must be randomly selected. The effect of stratification is to insure the proper representation of the entire population in the sample which is to be surveyed.

SYSTEMATIC TECHNIQUES

Systematic sampling may be less laborious than simple random sampling, but it has some pitfalls. To acquire a systematic sample from the entire population, each "nth" member is chosen for the sample. For example, if there are 1,000 members in the target population and 100 are to be surveyed, every 10th member is chosen, beginning with any number between one and ten. The starting number is randomly chosen from a listing of "n" numbers or from a table of random numbers. In the first example, a number would be randomly selected from numbers ranging from one to ten. If three were selected, then numbers in the sample would be 3, 13, 23, 33, . . . until 100 subjects were chosen.

To avoid biasing a sample when using the systematic sampling technique, the listing of the population must <u>not</u> be cyclically arranged. That is, it should not exhibit repeating patterns. For example, assume that 12 teachers from 12 elementary schools are to be surveyed. Each school has listed their teachers by grade level and each school has two classes for each of the grades, 1-6. If every 12th teacher were to be surveyed, and one be by selecting the second name and chose each 12th name thereafter, only first grade teachers could conceivably be surveyed. For this reason, attention must be given to the manner in which lists of the population are prepared to insure that cyclical patterns are not present which cause selection biases, and a nonrepresentative sample.

Sample Size

There are no absolute standards regarding the percentage of persons in a population who should be surveyed. However, it is imperative that those chosen be sufficiently representative of the entire population in the variables for which the sample will be analyzed. Perhaps "one rule of thumb" might be: On how small a group are you willing to gamble that their responses reflect all the others? Table 5-1 provides one estimate of the sample sizes needed for various populations. Please remember that the sizes are estimates and that each survey must be considered individually for its unique characteristics. No statistical inferences may be determined from the figures provided in Table 5-1.

Table 5-1. Estimated Population and Sample Sizes

Population Size	Sample Size	Population Size	Sample Size
100	79	5,000	357
200	132	6,000	361
300	168	8,000	367
400	196	10,000	370
500	217	15,000	375
600	234	20,000	377
800	260	30,000	379
1,000	278	50,000	381
2,000	322	75,000	382
3,000	341	100,000	383

Source: The National Education Association. Table 5-1 is reproduced with the written permission of the National Education Association.

Disproportional Sampling

In many cases, the distribution of the population will be such that the selection of a sample is based on the rationale that too few persons demonstrating a selected variable have any chance for drawing if a rigidly controlled stratified random sample is used. As an example, most surveys attempt to draw from known criteria, e.g., size of school or population of city. Observe the data in Table 5-2 from which a hypothetical (but typical) illustration will be developed.

Table 5-2. Hypothetical Population

Number of City Superintendents	Population of City
4	100,000 or higher
16	35,000 to 99,999
32	10,000 to 34,999
32	2,500 to 9,999
64	2,400 and fewer
Total 158	

If a stratified sample of 25% is to be drawn, then only one of the superintendents of the cities 100,000 or over would be selected. Not that bigness is goodness, but the bigger cities tend to set the pace for others. Knowing this potential, a researcher might decide to use a disproportionally selected, random sample. All 20 of the superintendents in cities 35,000 and larger might be selected, while 25% each from cities 2,500 to 34,999 would be selected. Perhaps a 20% sample would be drawn from the group in the population category 2,500 and fewer. Clearly such a disproportionate sample causes a bias in the favor of the larger groups. Yet, if the assumption were valid that the bigger cities tend to set the pace, and if such a design were not utilized, then the larger districts would not be represented adequately and the data might be erroneously biased for most of the districts.

Disproportionate samples are rather infrequently utilized in sampling. One problem is that the investigator might unconsciously make assumptions about the population which are not valid, thus tending to negate conclusions from the survey. However, where very few individuals exhibit a selection trait, this technique at least provides for a critical number to be sampled.

Lest one make a ridicule of this technique, it is similar to the method by which corporations determine the voting power of shareholders. The number of votes cast is contingent (albeit proportional) on the number of shares held--it is not one person, one equal vote! The same analogy might be prudently utilized for some samples: Not all respondents will be of equal power. When the data are analyzed, subgroup categories, of course, would be reported to determine similarities and differences between groups.

COMMUNICATING WITH THE TARGET POPULATION

Written Correspondence

Once the sample group has been selected, the next task is to insure that the participants receive and return the survey instrument. An effective cover letter explaining the reason for the study helps in the obtaining of a good return of the survey instrument. The cover letter explains the reason for the survey and why it is important for the respondent to personally complete the instrument. A well-written letter is a persuasive and motivating device.

The following points should be addressed when designing a cover letter:

1. State the purpose of the study clearly.
2. Explain the value of the study.
3. Explain how the data will be used.
4. Identify the sponsoring agency or institution.
5. Include the investigator's name and the name of the study's sponsor.
6. Give explicit directions for completing the questionnaire.
7. Provide a reasonable deadline for returning the questionnaire.
8. Assure the respondent that the data will be handled confidentially.

9. Ask if a copy of the results of the study are desired by the respondent.

10. Provide a self-addressed, stamped return envelope.

11. Date the letter.

12. Sign the letter personally.

13. Use an original or an extremely high quality copy.

A sample cover letter that contains all the points that have been mentioned above follows as Model 5-2. (See next page.)

Follow-Ups

The investigator usually conducts a follow-up after the initial mailing if the questionnaire return rate is not 100 percent. There are several methods that can be used. One technique is to send a second letter which "gently" requests cooperation in returning the questionnaire. Another method is to send a second questionnaire and return envelope with the second letter.

Postcards may also be used in the follow-up. With tight budgets, postcards are less expensive. A suggested postcard model is shown in Model 5-1 below.

Model 5-1. Suggested Postcard Follow-Up

Dear Vocational Educator:

Two weeks ago you received a questionnaire concerning vocational programs in your school. This is just a reminder to ask your help in completing and returning that questionnaire. If you have already done so, thank you. If not, your reply is needed to help in assessing vocational teacher supply and demand in the state.

Thank you for your cooperation.

Dr. Robyn A. Bird

Model 5-2. Sample Cover Letter

Rainier University
Side Hill Gouger, Washington 99469

Date

Dear Vocational Educator:

   The Office of Evaluation and Research at Rainier University, and the Public Schools, in cooperation with the Office of the Superintendent of Public Instruction, are conducting a study to assess the supply and demand of vocational teachers in this state. This information will be used for future planning by state colleges and universities.

   Enclosed is a questionnaire designed to complete the study. Your opinions are very much needed. Just mark the appropriate response for each item. If you would like to include comments of your own please write them in the Remarks section. All responses will be handled confidentially.

   We hope to complete the study by June 8th. Your cooperation will help us a great deal. If you want a copy of the completed study please so indicate on the questionnaire and we shall send it.

Sincerely yours,

Dr. Robyn A. Bird
Director of the Office of
   Evaluation and Research

Ms. Dianne L. Hunt
Project Assistant

RAB:ts

Enclosure: Questionnaire
               Return envelope

In general, you want a 100% return. If you have an adequate budget, use a telephone contact with tardy respondents. Therefore, you should follow-up with as many techniques as is possible. Your writer suggests the following set of procedures.

1. Mail the questionnaire--first mailing.
2. Within one week--mail a first follow-up postcard to all nonrespondents. (Some surveyors automatically mail a postcard to every sample member one week after the first mailing.
3. Within three weeks of the first mailing--send a second questionnaire, with a second cover letter stressing the importance of the instrument being returned.
4. Within one week of the mailing of the second instrument-- mail a second follow-up postcard.
5. Within two weeks of the second instrument--mail a third instrument.
6. Within one week of the third instrument--follow-up with a letter.
7. Last effort--telephone the nonrespondents.

If you follow the above system, you'll approach the 100% mark with every survey (assuming that it is a worthwile study). Remember, the closer you approach the 100% return goal, the more conclusive are your generalizations about the topic. There is no definite percent of returns which either "makes" or "breaks" a survey. If you are conducting the survey to make predictions about future events or decisions, then those future events will allow you to determine the effectiveness of the returns. Perhaps, reality is the ultimate test of survey results, but at least an 80% return is desirable, with 100% always being the goal.

Some suggestions that you should consider to obtain the maximum responses follow.

1. Is the entire questionnaire concise enough so that the respondent will not have to use time "guessing" what is required?

2. Will the subject be interesting to the respondent? If the subject of the investigation does not have any general interest, completed returns will be practically nil.

3. Is the questionnaire carefully designed (vocabulary, technical jargon) for a particular target population? You must know the language and vocabulary limitations of the clientele and create an instrument that can be understood by them.

4. Have the questions been printed with crisp, clean type? The physical appearance of the questionnaire can affect return rate. If the instrument has a messy appearance, it implies that the investigator will handle return data in an unprofessional manner.

5. Does the questionnaire look professional? Are the questions presented in an attractive, uncluttered way? An orderly presentation of items helps the respondent to reply more efficiently.

6. Is the questionnaire easy to handle? In other words, is the instrument void of loose inserts, fold-outs, and requirements to cross-reference particular items?

7. Are the directions for completing the questionnaire stated clearly? If a recipient is not afforded appropriate instructions on "how and what" to do, a large return cannot be expected.

From the respondent's point of view, the ease with which an instrument may be completed is very important to your attainment of a 100% return. The amount of involvement or interest that individuals have toward the topic may be inferred from the return rate.

Table 5-3 illustrates the percentage of returns received by Marjorie N. Donald after the initial mailing and subsequent follow-ups. By observing Donald's data, it may be seen that initial questionnaire return rates can be greatly increased with additional follow-ups.

Table 5-3. Percentage of Returns and Follow-up Techniques.*

Mailing or Follow-up	Percentage Returned
First mailing	46.2%
First follow-up letter	12.3%
Second follow-up letter plus second copy of questionnaire	8.8%
Telephone call plus third copy of the questionnaire if desired	10.1%
Total	77.4%

*From: Marjorie N. Donald, "Implications of Non-response for the Interpretation of Mail Questionnaire Data," Public Opinion Quarterly, Vol. 24, No. 1, 1960, p. 102. (Table 5-3 is abstracted from Donald's Table 1.)

However, observe the data presented in Table 5-4. By using biweekly mail follow-ups in a survey of vocational agriculture teachers, or the high school principals for schools without a vocational agriculture program, the percentage of responses was increased from 68 to 96! An additional one percent responded after telephone follow-ups, increasing the total response rate to 97 percent (Orlich and Rust).

The impact of nonrespondents can be determined by comparing "waves of respondents" (early, average, and slow returners). According to Larry L. Leslie (1972), if the population is rather homogeneous and if responses between waves do not differ, and if the sample is highly representative, then a very high response rate is probably not necessary.

In the study of vocational agriculture teachers, Orlich and Rust (1975, p. 3) analyzed the data received in the first two waves (second

Table 5-4. Questionnaire Response Waves and Follow-up Techniques

Dates (1975)	Activities	Questionnaires Returned		Questionnaires Outstanding	
		Number	Percent	Number	Percent
April 18	First Mailing to 311 Persons	0	0	311	100
April 30		202	65	109	35
May 2	-- WAVE I --	213	68	98	32
May 6	First Follow-up With Postcards to 98 Nonrespondents				
May 20	-- WAVE II --	236	76	75	24
May 22	Second Follow-up With New Letter And Another Copy of Questionnaire to 75 Nonrespondents				
June 3	-- WAVE III --	298	96	13	4
June 4	Telephone Calls to 13 Nonrespondents				
June 11	-- WAVE IV --	302	97	9	3

Data From: Donald C. Orlich and Gary A. Rust. *Supply and Demand for Vocational Agriculture Teachers in Washington State, 1975 and 1976.* Pullman: Washington State University, College of Education, Office of Field and Research Services, August 1975, 48 pp. (Data for Table 5-4 supplied from unpublished files.)

month of collection). No differences were observed in the patterns of responses between the two groups. The respondents in our survey apparently met the criterion of homogeneity which Leslie observed.

Ralph P. Stredwick (1972) surveyed 237 subjects using a disproportional random sample in seven Northwest public colleges and universities. By using four mail follow-ups, supplemented by a personal interview of the nonrespondents to the mail series, Stredwick received a total of 96.4 percent, or 228 responses from a sample of 237.

Summarizing a review of research on how to stimulate responses to mailed questionnaires, Arnold S. Linsky (1975) provided data which showed that mail follow-up techniques increased the responses from nonrespondents from 28 to 61 percent. Telephone follow-ups showed increases up to 83 percent.

Linsky identified several techniques which had been reported in the research literature that tended to increase response rates to mailed questionnaires. These, in part, were: (1) the use of a precontact letter prior to mailing the survey; (2) enclosure of a postcard to be returned by the respondent upon receipt of the instrument, simply stating that the questionnaire had arrived; (3) follow-ups of all types--postcards, letters, special delivery letters, telegrams, telephone calls, personal visits; (4) fixing a stamp to the return envelope rather than using a postage meter or permit number (a stamp seems to play psychologically on the frugal characteristics of people); and (5) preparation of a carefully written cover letter.

Collectively, these examples of follow-up techniques tend to support the wisdom that follow-up procedures do increase the response rates, and by rather large percentages. It is the responsibility of the investigator to obtain the largest possible percentage of returns. Every survey should have a large enough return of usable instruments so that the collective combined number of nonrespondents will not change the outcome of any critical item. The latter is a "big order." Yet, if the number of nonrespondents can offset respondent input, then the validity of the survey might be considered suspect. The implied assumption of your author is that there probably are differences between those who respond and those who chose not to respond. Let us explore that assumption.

Is the Nonrespondent a Factor?

A number of studies have analyzed the significance of nonresponses. Larry L. Leslie (1972) conducted a thorough study of nonresponse bias and concluded that: (1) when surveying populations with a common group identity (e.g., parents from one school, teachers in a school district), response differences between respondents, nonrespondents, and late respondents are unlikely; and (2) the most likely exception to the above is the case when the topic overrides the importance of group membership, e.g., highly personal or sensitive areas.

Contrariwise, Marjorie N. Donald (1960) found no significant demographic differences between respondents and nonrespondents in a study involving the members of League of Women Voters. Differences were found between respondents and nonrespondents on several traits, such as involvement in the organization and other demographic factors.

In 1970, Allan F. Williams and Henry Wechsler, however, demonstrated that even with homogeneous groups (dentists) there were significant differences between their survey respondents and nonrespondents.

F. L. Filion (1976) reported that nonrespondents to mail surveys do tend to bias the survey in favor of that group of the sample more actively involved in the topic which is being investigated. Suggesting that researchers analyze returns by "waves," Filion demonstrated that bias tendencies could be discovered. Comparisons of the returns by "wave" shows whether there are significant differences in response patterns. Filion used regression equations to predict nonrespondent bias.

If the potential exists for rather low return rates (assume under 75%) then multiple surveys might be designed for representative groups who are significant to the survey. Though the number or percent of response by group is low, the intensity of responses can be compared. By analyzing the various response categories, trends either supportive or antagonistic to the topics can be identified. Where there is convergence by various groups there may be a higher probability of making conclusions which tend to be supported. This technique was successfully used by your author in three separate vocational curriculum studies (Adams, Bennett, Knuteson, and Orlich, 1974). Contrariwise, if there is a divergence in responses among or between groups, then you might not desire to make conclusions, other than that there was divergence of opinion--a sorry comment, but the most prudent.

PROTECTION OF HUMAN SUBJECTS

Investigators at all levels must realize that recent federal regulations have placed limitations on methodologies which can be used when conducting research on human subjects, i.e., the participants.

Individuals who write proposals concerning behavioral, educational, or social research which will be submitted to the Department of Health, Education, and Welfare (D/HEW), or any other federal agency (and most state agencies) should be aware of legislation concerning the protection of human rights. Public Law 93-348, 1974, Title II, "Protection of Human Subjects of Biomedical and Behavioral Research," short title: "The National Research Service Award Act of 1974," establishes procedures that must be followed when any person is involved as a subject in any behavioral studies program funded by D/HEW or any other federal agency!

The law is lengthy and technical. For your purposes, it is necessary to know that a National Commission for the Protection of Human Subjects of Biomedical and Behavioral Research has been established. Its duties include establishing guidelines for biomedical and behavioral research to protect human rights. The Commission's responsibility entails developing methods for evaluation and monitoring the performance of institutional review boards. Also, the Commission investigates biomedical and behavioral research conducted or supported under HEW programs involving children, prisoners, and institutionalized mentally infirm persons.

The Assistant Secretary for Planning and Evaluation (D/HEW) established rules for the protection of the privacy of persons who are the subjects of projects sponsored by D/HEW. The following excerpt from the Federal Register is very explicit and illustrates the kinds of constraints placed on human research, a category which would include most surveys.

. . . .

(c) Protection of privacy. (1) No project supported under this part may involve the use of a data collection instrument which constitute [sic] invasions of personal privacy through inquiries regarding such matters as religion, sex, race, or politics. (2) A grantee which proposes to use a data collection instrument shall set forth in the grant application an explanation of the safeguards which will be used to restrict the use and disclosure of information so obtained to purposes directly connected with the project, including provisions for the destruction of such instruments where no longer needed for the purposes of the project.

(d) Clearance of instruments. (1) Grantees will not be required to submit data-collecting instruments to the Assistant Secretary or obtain the Assistant Secretary's approval for the use of these instruments, except where the notification of grant award specifically so provides. (2) If a grantee is required under paragraph (d) (1) of this section to submit data-collection instruments for the approval of the Assistant Secretary or if a grantee wishes the Assistant Secretary to review a data-collection instrument, the grantee shall submit seven copies of the document to the Assistant Secretary along with seven copies of the Office of Management and Budget's standard form No. 83 and seven copies of the Supporting Statement as required in the "Instructions for Requesting OMB Approval under the Federal Reports Act (Standard form No. 83A). (Federal Register, p. 1518.)

. . . .

All colleges and universities have established "Institutional Review Boards" specifically for the purpose of protecting subjects and helping researchers design experiments or data collection systems that do not infringe the rights of the respondents. Lest those of you who conduct surveys for advanced degrees feel that your surveys are beyond such jurisdiction, be assured that they ARE NOT! This means that after your final instrument has been approved by some research or thesis committee, it must be screened by the appropriate Institutional Review Board! In most cases--where sensitive information is not collected--there will be little or no cause for design change. If you plan to collect sensitive information, i.e., about religion, sex, race, or politics, then you must meet the standards established by the respective institution AND you must submit your instrument and research design for review. This regulation also applies to the use of copyrighted and/or published tests on instruments.

Do not hesitate to seek clarification from the Graduate School of your respective institution if you are associated with a college or university. If unattached, and information is required, then contact any of the regional department field offices of the U.S. Department of Health, Education, and Welfare.

The survey "game" is becoming a bit more complicated. It behooves you to become familiar with the guidelines concerning the privacy and protection of human subjects.

INCLUSIONARY LANGUAGE

Another consideration when writing data-gathering instruments, cover letters, or final reports is to use inclusionary language. Inclusionary language helps to remove sex bias in dialogues or in reports. The designers of survey instruments must also illustrate sensitivity to this emerging societal concern. The following statements are offered as comparative samples.

> Example 1. "After a student completes the chemistry course, he will be able to use three different methods to compute pH's."

The implication of this statement is that females do not take chemistry courses. The statement could have been improved if it had been written with inclusionary language:

> Example 2. "Upon completion of the chemistry course, students will be able to use three different methods to compute pH."

Example 3. "Upon completion of the Family Living module, <u>she</u> will be able to plan a weekly budget."

Again, this implies that males have no desire to be involved with a course in Family Living. The more appropriate writing would be:

Example 4. "Upon completion of the Family Living module, the participant will be able to plan a weekly budget."

Other Examples

When writing cover letters or follow-up letters use alternatives for the traditional "Dear Sir:" when the sex of the addressee is unknown. Other salutations that could be used include: Dear "Supervisor," "Director," "Owner," "Faculty Member," or "Dear Educator." There are also alternatives that may be used when describing various vocations such as "letter carrier" instead of "mailman," "human resources" instead of "manpower," and "newscaster" instead of "newsman."

It takes just a few moments and some cognitive awareness to rephrase most sex-role oriented items. Rather than writing he or she, use generic terms--student, respondent, participant. As the awareness and demand for the use of inclusionary language become more widespread, it would not be surprising to observe questionnaires being returned, unmarked, with a scribbled statement--"You did not use inclusionary language." Save yourself from a "touchy" communications problem. Write the entire study using inclusionary language.

"Where do you get models," you ask?

<u>My dear reader, this entire book may be considered the model!</u>

ONE PLANNING TECHNIQUE

Since planning is stressed so intently by the author, it seems appropriate to include at least one planning guide in the form of a PERT Network (Program Evaluation and Review Technique). The network illustrated in Figure 5-3 displays the many events and a set of possible sequences needed to conduct a "typical" survey. Depending on the survey's complexity, elements may be deleted, added, or expanded. By considering all possible events before the survey is conducted, you are able to anticipate personnel, time, and material needs. In addition, a PERT chart helps you to anticipate problem areas that could interfere with the successful fruition of the project.

The "tips" presented in this chapter should aid in the overall conduct of a survey. Conducting any survey is a rigorous and serious effort--not something that is hastily constructed and distributed.

The emphasis thus far has been on rather traditional questionnaire surveys or designs. Chapter 6 presents some instrumentation techniques and modifications that may provide creative designs that you may have not previously considered as having the potential of being questionnaires.

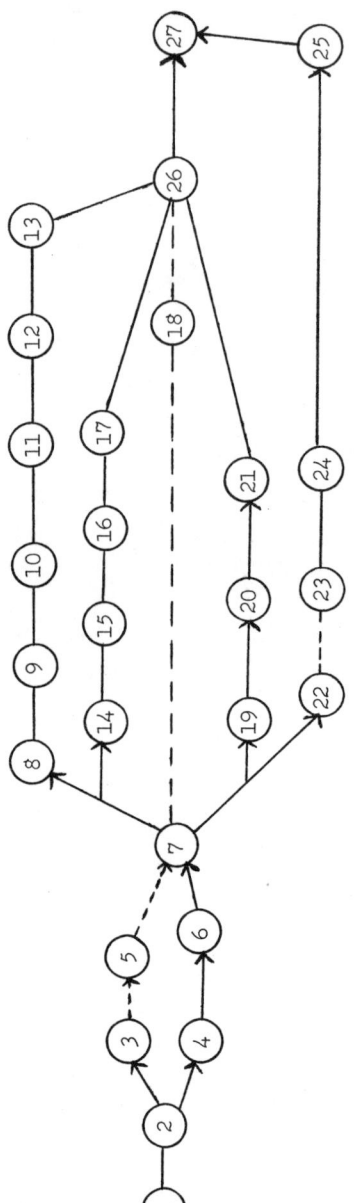

Figure 5-3. PERT Network for "Typical" Survey Project

1. Decision to "Go"
2. Complete Purpose/Goals/ Hypotheses
3. Determine Data Needs
4. State Objectives
5. Review Related Literature
6. Begin Item Construction
7. Review by Data Processing Consultant
8. Obtain Endorsements
9. Identify Universe Population
10. Design Sampling Technique
11. Begin Sample Selection
12. Complete Sample List
13. Complete Mailing Materials
14. Complete Instrument
15. Pilot Test Instrument
16. Revise Instrument
17. Prepare Final Form
18. Complete Administrative Procedures
19. Design Methods of Tabulation
20. Plan Analytic Techniques
21. Select Statistical Tests
22. Select Interviewers
23. Complete Interviewer Selection
24. Train Interviewers
25. Start Field Interviews
26. Mail Questionnaires
27. Tabulate Initial Returns

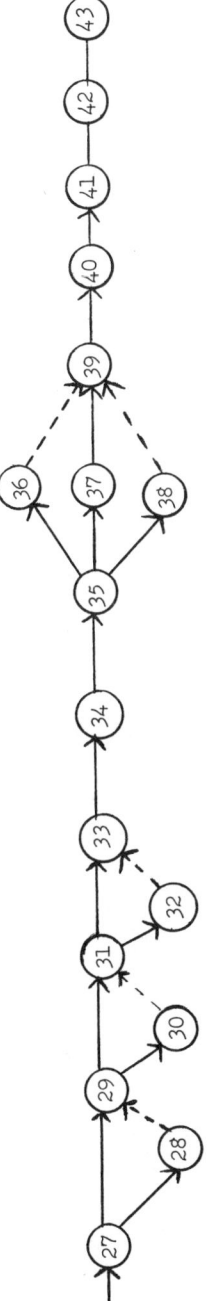

Figure 5-3, Continued. PERT Network for Survey Project

27. Tabulate Initial Returns
28. Send First Follow-up
29. Tabulate Returns
30. Send Second Follow-up
31. Tabulate Returns
32. Send Final Follow-up
33. Final Tabulations of Returns
34. Begin Statistical Tests
35. Complete Statistical Tests
36. Interpret Results
37. Prepare Tables
38. Prepare Figures
39. Test Hypotheses
40. Begin Final Report
41. Complete Final Report
42. Publish Results
43. Act

107

CHAPTER 6

Adapting Other Designs

The preceeding chapters emphasized the "basics" of questionnaire construction--communication, precision, objectivity, simplicity, and clarity. The usual designs of the previously described instruments are rather traditional. There are, however, other information-gathering techniques which may be of value as alternate models or as component parts of a survey. Included in this group are the Delphi technique, adapting statements of intended policy as items, "needs" surveys, and "couplet" design. Each is developed further.

OTHER EFFECTIVE METHODS

Delphi Technique

The Delphi technique was originally developed and popularized by the RAND Corporation (Helmer, 1967). RAND developed the technique as a method of identifying group opinions, initially about defense needs, and named it the "Delphi" method to honor the great oracle of Apollo. Basically, the respondents participate in three or more rounds of surveying, where they receive their own data and the data for the entire group prior to each round. Delphi provides a continual system for feedback to all participants, but through a privileged design. The Delphi technique is justified primarily on the rationale that it: allows for professional judgments to be made, avoids personality conflicts and interpersonal politics, and reduces the impact of status or high position persons from forcing judgments in group discussions in the direction which they deem desirable. The Delphi method is one means to identify organizational consensus, identify problem areas, or to prioritize goals by providing detailed feedback and systematic follow-up.

One of the problems in making decisions is to forecast or predict what the future might hold. Or, it may be prudent to prioritize goals which have already been identified through a needs assessment or opinionnaire. To this end the "Delphi Technique" allows a methodology for organizing and prioritizing the collective judgments of the polled group or those who are concerned with the planning and implementing of change. This technique is an excellent way to seek inputs on what may be causes or effects in problem solution.

The initial procedure is to prepare, distribute, and synthesize a series of questions or problem statements for evaluation. For example, one may distribute a questionnaire which contains a series of problems, statements, opinions, activities, or predictions of future probabilities. Obtained from the first round is a rank ordering, prioritizing, or evaluating of each item. A modification of that first step is to prepare a generalized statement which elicits specific respondent statements which are ultimately converted to items for judging, similar to that initially noted.

All selected participants receive a second listing of items and are asked to either rate the list by selected criteria or to re-evaluate their original listing in consideration of the responses provided from the initial ranking. Depending on the method of initiation, the lists are returned to each respective respondent with a detailed list of rankings, plus adverse comments, new ideas for consideration and minority reports. Typically, the group mean or mode <u>per item</u> is computed and fed back to all participants.

The tabulator of the instruments reanalyzes the data and prepares yet another (third) instrument for redistribution to the selected sample.

This procedure continues through at least four rankings. By using multiple submissions of the same set of data each respondent reaffirms original opinions, modifies some, or adds additional items to the list. The technique aids in the forming of a clearly defined convergence pattern of major points, plus a well-outlined minority opinion.

The Delphi technique is easily adaptable to surveys which are designed to analyze the instituting of innovative programs, problems, or opinions. A series of events might be rated as to their desirability or probability of occurring. In addition, all respondents are encouraged to provide statements about the impact that events might bring if they do occur. For example, the Delphi technique is most effective in first determining whether or not a group can identify issues, concerns, problems, or suggested courses of action.

Another organizational problem--the formulation of educational policies and plans which allow for alternative future options--can be solved by Delphi analyses. In such cases, preference statements could be written by a task force. The list could then be distributed to the selected subgroup for their initial responses. The complete Delphi technique would then follow. Consensus can easily be identified for those items which have the higher or lower means or modes.

In one sense, the Delphi technique is not a scientific technique, but **rather** a feedback mechanism by which selected members of an organization **have an** effect in shaping organizational goals and policies. It is a very **systematic** method, nevertheless.

One example. The "Suggested Goals for Washington Common Schools," published in September, 1971, by the Washington State Board of Education, were synthesized from data obtained by the Delphi technique. During the spring of 1971, a wide geographic and occupational cross-section of 866 Washington citizens was identified to participate in a three-phase Delphi survey. The sample survey was comprised of urban, suburban, and rural area persons and included teachers, administrators, students, business people, labor leaders, professionals, persons involved in higher education, and staff members of the State Superintendent of Public Instruction (SSPI).

The selected respondents were first asked to prognosticate about the decade of the 1970s and to share their thinking and feelings about what students ought to know, feel, and be able to do as a result of their K-12 school experiences. As responses were gathered, consensus opinions and dissenting opinions were studied carefully and ultimately used to develop Washington's "Ten Goals for the Common Schools." Of interest, the minority opinions which were obtained in this manner numbered 67 (with accompanying subgroups) and were published as a statement of the SSPI entitled, "Delphi Survey Minority Opinion Report," on July 10, 1971. Thus, the Delphi technique has been utilized to identify both majority and minority consensus positions for a state educational system.

Alfred F. Rasp (1974) reported that through the Washington Delphi survey both proponent and opponent groups were identified for selected policy statements. By subdividing the respondents into seven occupational categories, Rasp was able to determine participation rates in the survey, "tenacity" rates (i.e., the ease or reluctance to abandon original priorities), and a profile of priorities by respondent group. See Table 6-1 for a set of selected items from the Washington Delphi Survey and other model items.

Advantages of the Delphi. Through the use of repeated questionnaires, issues tend to become clarified; thus an investigator can determine critical, short, and long range concerns from the more ephemeral ones. Group consensus is gained through each subsequent issuance of the instrument, allowing each individual to reexamine the original position and reconsider whether there is need for a change in position based on information about group behavior. Supportive and opposition elements within the organization are made known. Such data aids in the implementing of programs or the postponing of the same, if internal support is needed or lacking. Priorities are clearly identified. In short, the Delphi technique is a powerful tool by which information is gathered for planning and decision-making.

Disadvantages of the Delphi. It might be assumed that the Delphi technique would readily identify problem areas or conflicting opinions and attitudes with great ease. However, when there is a lack of clear consensus, the method used in making the rankings might, in fact, shift the priorities. Several techniques may be used to determine arithmetical scales, such as (1) total weighted average, (2) median ranking, (3) frequency rankings, (4) unweighted frequency, or (5) rank orders. In determining the weights of a Delphi survey, Dr. Toshio Akamine, a colleague of the author, noted that items would shift upward or downward in priority, depending on the ranking method being used. In this particular case, the top and bottom items remained in those positions, respectively, regardless of method used. But the other six items, especially the second, third, and fourth, shifted about. Akamine's observation illustrates a subjective characteristic

Table 6-1. Ten Selected Final Responses from the
State of Washington Delphi Survey to Determine Goals for Common Schools*

July 10, 1971

The left-hand column shows the modal responses for each item in brackets.

The scale of priority is: 1 2 3 4 5 6

1 = Schools ought not be involved   2 = Lowest priority   3 = Low priority

4 = Some priority--after higher priorities are achieved   5 = High priority   6 = High priority-- a must

---

Response Priorities**   Selected Items

                              As a result of the experiences provided by the public
                              common school system, each student should:

Lowest   Highest
1 2 3 4 [5] 6   Have an understanding of alternative political and economic systems.

1 2 3 4   5 [6]   Demonstrate competency in the basic skills commonly known as the 3 R's.

1 2 3 4 [5] 6   Be able to read the daily newspaper with understanding.

1 2 3 [4] 5   6   Be able to compare the basic beliefs of the major world religions.

1 2 [3] 4   5   6   Be able to develop logical proofs in geometry.

1] 2 3 4   5   6   Understand the importance of and be willing to participate in nonviolent demonstrations.

1 2 3 [4] 5   6   Be able to "kill time" in a way that is personally satisfying.

1] 2 3 4   5   6   Develop an ability to "beat the system."

1 2 3 4 [5] 6   Possess a commitment to the American way of life.

1 2 3 4   5 [6]   Know and apply the principles of safe driving.

---

*Of interest to researchers, the means, medians, and modes of each of the 67 items on the final list all coincided respectively and are shown enclosed in [ ]. This feature shows the power of the Delphi method to shape respondent consensus.

**The 10 items above are examples and do not have any implied prioritizing.

of the Delphi technique as one attempts to quantify responses. It is not to be construed that the Delphi technique is not a powerful tool. This analysis points out that there is a problem in ranking the items when one attempts to quantify them and reduce bias.

A second major concern and problem which appears when using the Delphi technique is that the manner in which the statements are written affects the priority rankings. Value-laden terms cause a shifting in rank upward or downward. It becomes extremely crucial that statements be either value-free, or reflect precise points. This is not to state that value-laden items ought not be included. But if included, value-laden items may cause a biased set of responses.

Stating or developing an initial set of items could be a problem. To begin with, all selected respondents have some "intuitive" or "felt" concerns. It may be well to begin with these concerns. Or it may be better to begin with an open-ended response questionnaire where all respondents are asked to list or identify what they consider to be the two or three major problems associated with the survey topic (as was done in Washington). These lists would then be sent to an editing group for compilation. However, if the lists are very lengthy, then additional editing, classifying, and grouping must take place so that a meaningful response pattern can be generated when the first questionnaire is distributed to the respondents. Subjectivity may enter into the editing of initial or added statements.

One last caution--the lists which may be generated by a group may be very biased from the inception. This means that valid causes or positions might not even be listed by respondents. If a major policy determination is to be accomplished via the Delphi technique, it may be prudent to retain an outside consultant to analyze each of the statements for implied meanings, as well as to identify statements or priorities that were not explicitly identified.

As minority opinions are appended to the basic questionnaire, the chances of their moving up to top priorities are highly improbable if only three distributions of the questionnaire are made. If one uses the Delphi technique, and desires to have the minority opinions appended with an opportunity for prioritizing, then <u>a minimum of four</u> questionnaires must be distributed. The second questionnaire would contain the minority items for the first time. The third questionnaire would show how respondents ranked the minority items, while the fourth questionnaire would require further ranking and evaluating by respondents. Your writer's personal experience has shown that <u>no</u> minority item ever moved into the top priority areas.

The Delphi technique requires at least one month or longer to accomplish, depending on the size of the group and the complexity of questionnaire responses. The important consideration is that the selected sample has an opportunity to identify those issues or problems which it perceives as important. Further, this method allows administrators to add their input since they too are concerned with the problems which will occur as changes take place in programs. Administrators may desire to send out their own Delphi questionnaire to identify administrative priorities.

As a survey technique, the Delphi method has proven to be of valuable assistance in decision-making.

Adapting Statements of Intended Policy

When long range priorities are being formulated, there is often a concomitant distribution of policy statements or position papers which describes the rationale, implementation factors, or operational procedures. How does one obtain objective critiques or feedback concerning this common administrative <u>modus operandi</u>? One simple technique is to abstract the main points from the appropriate documents--even quoting directly where possible--and to use these statements as the items for a questionnaire, or as the items for a Delphi survey.

This technique is most applicable when attempting to determine the attitudes of affected users or, as in the case of schools, when new programs are being planned or when new curricula or textbooks are being adopted. In these cases, a committee might objectively prepare a series of statements which accurately portrays the program or textbook and distribute the items in survey format to the teachers who will ultimately teach the program. It is the prudent administrator who conducts a survey based on statements synthesized from the intended program, when major innovations are being planned or the implementation of a major innovation is highly probable.

As one example, the decade between 1967 and 1976 gave rise to several elementary and secondary school science programs which emphasized "processes" of science, rather than "contents" of science. The newer programs tended to require: (1) inductive logic, (2) hands-on experiences for children, (3) inquiry techniques, (4) observational-evaluation systems, and (5) utilization of a consistent learning theory. "Traditional" teachers (whoever they may be) usually needed extensive inservice education programs to implement successfully the above selected set of teaching competencies which were assumed by program developers.

Teachers are not totally against change, but, when a school district's curriculum committee votes to adopt such new programs, the more successful adoptors do, in fact, conduct surveys of the teachers to determine receptivity and to identify areas that need additional school support--inservice activities, purchase of expendable materials, resource centers. By using statements which reflect the proposed programs, the surveys identify the relative support or opposition to the intended program activities. See Model 6-1 for one example.

Model 6-1 illustrates only a partial listing of the necessary items that must be included in a science education survey. (Note: The format is adapted to data processing through its numbering system.) If such a questionnaire were to be distributed, it would be best to establish a series of categories in which all appropriate items might be classified. The general categories should include:

1. Teaching styles and methodologies.
2. Student perceptions of science.
3. Teacher perceptions about science instruction.
4. Evaluation of student progress.
5. Materials and equipment.
6. Management strategies.
7. Inservice education.
8. Basic orientation--text, activities, combinations.
9. Evaluation of the program, per se.

Model 6-1. Partial Science Survey

SCIENCE SURVEY

1. Please indicate the grade level in which you teach by checking only <u>one</u> of the categories.

   ___ 1.1 Grade One   ___ 1.4 Grade Four   ___ 1.7 Grade Seven
   ___ 1.2 Grade Two   ___ 1.5 Grade Five   ___ 1.8 Grade Eight
   ___ 1.3 Grade Three   ___ 1.6 Grade Six   ___ 1.9 Other (specify)

On the scale at the right, please circle the number that best describes your reaction to each statement.

	Strongly Agree	Agree	No Opinion	Disagree	Strongly Disagree
2. Children in my school grade enjoy science.	5	4	3	2	1
3. A good science program provides hands-on materials that are adaptable to varied teacher and student needs.	5	4	3	2	1
4. Our district should adopt an activity-centered science program.	5	4	3	2	1
5. A good science program teaches students the principles discovered by scientists during the past years.	5	4	3	2	1
6. Our school district should adopt a science program which has a combination of text readings and hands-on activities for students.	5	4	3	2	1
7. When our district adopts a new science program, an in-service training program for teachers should be provided.	5	4	3	2	1
8. I enjoy teaching science.	5	4	3	2	1
9. I feel that my preparation for inquiry techniques as related to science teaching is ample.	5	4	3	2	1

By organizing the survey into a series of distinct categories, the results may be tabulated so that each section is assigned a ratio based on an average of coded responses. In this manner, areas of critical need are identified. Such a survey might include at least 50 items.

If the district had already adopted a program and still desired to have additional input from the teachers to determine strengths and weaknesses, or areas that need development for intensive in-service education, then the statements for the survey could be adapted directly from the teacher's manual or the program prospectus.

The possibility for using adapted statements of intended policy as survey items has virtually unlimited application.

Needs Surveys

One of the more popular uses of surveys at the local school district level is the conduct of "needs" surveys. Through the systematic collection of opinions from students, teachers, administrators, patrons, parents, and citizens, school district decision-makers are able to determine the support and opposition to probable programs, activities, or goals. There is really no limitation to the kinds of needs surveys which may be conducted. Among the topics included in them are: (1) attitudes toward school building needs, (2) attitudes toward changing school boundaries, school openings, or closings, (3) opinions about goals and program desires, (4) probable support for school levies, (5) possible curriculum expansions or deletions, (6) anticipated evaluation methods, (7) determination of long range priorities; and many, many more.

Why the rather renewed emphasis and upsurge on these types of planning surveys? In your author's opinion, the emergence of needs surveys illustrates the desire of decision-makers to reflect more accurately all of their constituencies. Needs assessments provide one means by which the schools and their supporting communities might become more supportive of each other. Further, needs assessments provide valuable data so that future decisions might be made more prudently and with acknowledged community support.

Further, with the advent of "categorical federal aid" to school districts, there is the necessity to comply with federal regulations--one of which is the demonstration of need for the aid.

The conduct of a survey is not always mandatory to determine needs for specific groups. If the children are tested with valid and reliable tests, then the scores of these measures can be used to determine one component of intellectual needs--in the form of greater emphasis on some topic or skill. Demographic, socio-economic, geographic, and other relevant data can be collected from primary or secondary sources to support an "emerging" need. Yet, there are many topics or concerns in which the only method for collecting data is the needs survey.

An example for in-service needs. One of the problems confronting most administrators or program specialists is the continual necessity for staff development, or in-service education. As programs change and as knowledge is expanded, teachers and administrators at all levels must continue to improve their knowledge and skills or simply find themselves becoming obsolete. This "fact" of schooling is not only a national one, but also has international implications. To illustrate one technique, your author is adapting and selecting items which were used by the East Asian Regional Council of Overseas Schools in a recent needs survey focusing on in-service desires for both administrators and teachers.

As you examine Models 6-2 and 6-3 note how the survey instrument attempts to identify the areas of greatest perceived need and the priorities which respondents attach to those self-identified needs. These models are easily adapted to any school or district. Further, by changing the numbering systems, all items are transferable to electronic data processing systems.

By using separate survey forms for each group, relevant data are obtained from the respective individuals. The technique of designing a distinct instrument for each client group is one with great applicability. It is often useful to print the different instruments on different colors of paper for ease of identification.

After the tabulations are made and reported to the appropriate agency or administrator, decisions may be made about immediate staff training needs-- based on the perceptions of those who are directly involved. What better way to assure that the in-service programs will be supported by the intended group?

Model 6-2. Abstracted Administrator Needs Assessment Instrument

The Council desires to provide relevant administrator staff development activities. To aid in planning that process, an instrument has been developed to elicit specific responses to specific topics. You will note that the items in the far left-hand column list specific topics related to administration. The column entitled "Your Proficiency" asks for your own evaluation of your proficiency for each specified topic. "Your Desire" asks for opinions of your intention to learn more about the selected administrative topic. The final column, "Your Priority," is to be used to indicate the FIRST or top priority within each group.

For your ease of response, circle the number which is coded for each of the three areas. Each rating scale is described below.

YOUR PROFICIENCY

1 -- Indicates that you already know of the topic and are using it.
2 -- Indicates that you know of the topic, but do not use it.
3 -- Indicates that you are not knowledgeable of that topic.

YOUR DESIRE

1 -- Indicates that you ARE desirous of becoming proficient to use that topic in your administration.
2 -- Indicates that you are NOT desirous of becoming proficient to use the specific topic in your administration.

YOUR PRIORITY

1 -- Indicates YOUR HIGHEST priority to attend a staff development program for that topic.

RANK ORDER ONLY THE TOP PRIORITY ITEM FOR EACH OF THE MAJOR SECTIONS OF THE IDENTIFIED TOPICS.

Please circle your proficiency, AND your desire for each specific topic. Do not omit any items. Circle a "1" in the far right column to indicate your highest priority for staff development programs within each major section. This technique allows you to identify your administrative strengths and to identify areas for future professional growth. The prioritizing allows you to establish your true "wants."

TOPICS	Your Rated Proficiency for Each Topic			Your Desire to Know More about Each Topic		Specify Your Highest Priority by circling only one of the numbers below
Section I	1 Know & Use	2 Known, but Not Used	3 Not Known	1 Desired	2 Not Desired	
PERSONAL MANAGEMENT STYLES						
Change Agent Concept	1	2	3	1	2	1
Communications	1	2	3	1	2	1
Enabling Behaviors	1	2	3	1	2	1
Interaction Analysis	1	2	3	1	2	1
Problem-Solving	1	2	3	1	2	1
Other--Specify	1	2	3	1	2	1

TOPICS	Your Rated Proficiency for Each Topic			Your Desire to Know More about Each Topic		Specify Your Highest Priority by circling only one of the numbers below
Section II	1 Know & Use	2 Known, but Not Used	3 Not Known	1 Desired	2 Not Desired	
MANAGEMENT PLANNING SKILLS						
Delphi Technique	1	2	3	1	2	1
Management by Objective (MBO)	1	2	3	1	2	1
Planning, Programming, Budgeting (PPBS)	1	2	3	1	2	1
Program Evaluation Review Technique (PERT)	1	2	3	1	2	1
Other--Specify	1	2	3	1	2	1

Model 6-3. Abstracted Teacher Needs Assessment Instrument*

TOPICS	Your Rated Proficiency for Each Topic			Your Desire to Know More about Each Topic		Specify Your Highest Priority by circling or one of the numbers below
Section I	1 Know & Use	2 Known, but Not Used	3 Not Known	1 Desired	2 Not Desired	
TEACHING TECHNOLOGIES						
Audio-tutorial Systems	1	2	3	1	2	1
Behavior Modification	1	2	3	1	2	1
Criterion Referenced Evaluation	1	2	3	1	2	1
Flanders Interaction Analysis System	1	2	3	1	2	1
Individualized Instruction	1	2	3	1	2	1
Learning Activity Packages (LAPS)	1	2	3	1	2	1
Performance Objectives	1	2	3	1	2	1
Precision Teaching	1	2	3	1	2	1
Programmed Instruction	1	2	3	1	2	1
Other--Specify	1	2	3	1	2	1

*Directions are omitted from Model 6-3. They would be almost identical to those shown for Model 6-2.

TOPICS	Your Rated Proficiency for Each Topic			Your Desire to Know More about Each Topic		Specify Your Highest Priority by circling only one of the numbers below
Section II	1 Know & Use	2 Known, but Not Used	3 Not Known	1 Desired	2 Not Desired	
TEACHING METHODS						
Classroom Management	1	2	3	1	2	1
Discussion-leading Models	1	2	3	1	2	1
Inquiry Techniques	1	2	3	1	2	1
Questioning Strategies	1	2	3	1	2	1
Other--Specify	1	2	3	1	2	1

Couplet Designs

One of the major uses of survey data is to determine how "strongly" selected respondents feel about the topics on which the questionnaire is focused. To accomplish this task, designers tend to repeat one or more key questions throughout the instrument. Repetitious statements often cause respondents to omit several items. The investigator thus loses valuable data and the conclusions to be drawn from the study tend to be far more tentative than one might desire, if not invalid.

Studying a problem with similar characteristics, Frank B. McMahon, Jr., (1969), a psychologist, desired to eliminate the ambiguity of items used in selected psychological tests. To accomplish greater precision, he added a qualifying or amplifying statement after each basic item. Thus, McMahon invented the "couplet" question for psychological tests. As he wrote in 1969, if a respondent reacts in the same direction to both the item and the couplet portion, then that respondent truly acknowledges that the item reflects a problem that, "is important enough to admit to twice," (McMahon, p. 57).

McMahon's couplet technique has direct applicability to survey designs. Rather than trying to mask questions in the survey to determine strength of response or strong feelings about a topic, you can simply adapt a couplet design. For example, assume that you wanted to know attitudes about science in the elementary school, then the couplet might be prepared as follows:

	Agree	Undecided	Disagree
1. To what extent do you agree that science should be taught in the elementary school?	3	2	1

	Agree	Undecided	Disagree
1.a. If you agreed with the statement, then do you agree that science should be considered a "basic" with reading, writing and arithmetic--the traditional "three R's"?	3	2	1

Note the simple and forward construction of the question. This design allows a clarification of respondent feelings immediately. Such a design eliminates the need for "reverse" items, which were previously discussed.

An adaptor of the couplet design was Gail Catherine McClay (1976), who conducted a survey among curriculum innovators and implementors. She identified eight major roles which could be differentiated between implementors and initiators of educational innovations. McClay provided her respondents with three options and a series of related items for any of three possible responses--agree, undecided, disagree. Observe Model 6-4 which presents her unique adaptation of McMahon's couplet design to a quintuplet.

Through the use of couplet designs, a questionnaire may be reduced in size, and yet focus on problems or issues with greater precision and fewer questions than is possible with the traditionally designed questionnaire.*

---

*Permission to illustrate and modify couplet design is granted with the written permission of Frank B. McMahon, Jr.

Model 6-4. Selected Illustration of Modified Couplet
Design for Surveys*

IMPLEMENTOR QUESTIONNAIRE

A. THE ROLE OF THE IMPLEMENTOR OF EDUCATIONAL INNOVATION IS <u>NOT</u> SIMILAR TO ROLE OF THE INITIATOR OF EDUCATIONAL INNOVATION.

AGREE ___
UNDECIDED ___
DISAGREE ___

IF YOU AGREE WITH CONCEPT A, PLEASE ANSWER NUMBERS 1, 2, 3, 4, 5 and 16.

1. The role of the implementor is to implement programs in the classroom, rather than to search for innovative program information and research.

STRONGLY AGREE ___ MILDLY AGREE ___ UNCERTAIN ___ MILDLY DISAGREE ___ STRONGLY DISAGREE ___

2. The role of the implementor is one of involvement with the teachers and students in a particular educational setting, rather than with researching ideas applicable to that setting.

STRONGLY AGREE ___ MILDLY AGREE ___ UNCERTAIN ___ MILDLY DISAGREE ___ STRONGLY DISAGREE ___

3. The role of the implementor is one of finalizing the change process for a specific innovation, rather than starting the change process.

STRONGLY AGREE ___ MILDLY AGREE ___ UNCERTAIN ___ MILDLY DISAGREE ___ STRONGLY DISAGREE ___

4. The role of the implementor is evidenced by his/her place within the school organization rather than with the total structure of the district.

STRONGLY AGREE ___ MILDLY AGREE ___ UNCERTAIN ___ MILDLY DISAGREE ___ STRONGLY DISAGREE ___

5. The role of the implementor is one of adapting his/her behavior to facilitate innovative implementation, rather than to direct others in behavior change.

STRONGLY AGREE ___ MILDLY AGREE ___ UNCERTAIN ___ MILDLY DISAGREE ___ STRONGLY DISAGREE ___

*Source: Gail Catherine McClay, "Perceived Role Differentiation and Congruency Among Implementors and Initiators of Educational Innovation." Unpublished Doctoral Dissertation, Washington State University, Pullman, pp. 124-125, 1976. Printed with written permission from Gail C. McClay.

IF YOU DISAGREE WITH CONCEPT A, PLEASE ANSWER NUMBERS 6, 7, 8, 9, 10 and 16.

6. The role of the implementor is to understand the initiation phase of a specific innovation.

STRONGLY AGREE ____ MILDLY AGREE ____ UNCERTAIN ____ MILDLY DISAGREE ____ STRONGLY DISAGREE ____

7. The same process involved in the implementation phase is involved in the initiation phase of the change process.

STRONGLY AGREE ____ MILDLY AGREE ____ UNCERTAIN ____ MILDLY DISAGREE ____ STRONGLY DISAGREE ____

8. The role of the implementor is to understand the personal orientation of the initiator role.

STRONGLY AGREE ____ MILDLY AGREE ____ UNCERTAIN ____ MILDLY DISAGREE ____ STRONGLY DISAGREE ____

9. The role of the implementor should include the willingness to try the further initiation of the specific innovation in his/her school setting.

STRONGLY AGREE ____ MILDLY AGREE ____ UNCERTAIN ____ MILDLY DISAGREE ____ STRONGLY DISAGREE ____

10. The motivation for the implementation of a specific innovation is similar to the motivation for the initiation of that same innovation.

STRONGLY AGREE ____ MILDLY AGREE ____ UNCERTAIN ____ MILDLY DISAGREE ____ STRONGLY DISAGREE ____

IF YOU ARE UNDECIDED ABOUT CONCEPT A, PLEASE ANSWER NUMBERS 11, 12, 13, 14, 15, and 16.

11. I have insufficient knowledge of the initiator's role to make a judgment about role similarity.

STRONGLY AGREE ____ MILDLY AGREE ____ UNCERTAIN ____ MILDLY DISAGREE ____ STRONGLY DISAGREE ____

12. My involvement with the change process has been restricted to the implementation level.

STRONGLY AGREE ____ MILDLY AGREE ____ UNCERTAIN ____ MILDLY DISAGREE ____ STRONGLY DISAGREE ____

13. The information of which I am aware about role similarity between initiators and implementors of educational innovation is insufficient for me to make a judgment.

STRONGLY AGREE ____   MILDLY AGREE ____   UNCERTAIN ____   MILDLY DISAGREE ____   STRONGLY DISAGREE ____

14. There is insufficient evidence to show that perceived role similarity would enhance or impede the implementation of educational innovation.

STRONGLY AGREE ____   MILDLY AGREE ____   UNCERTAIN ____   MILDLY DISAGREE ____   STRONGLY DISAGREE ____

15. I have not had sufficient contact with initiators of educational innovation to make decisions about their mode of operation.

STRONGLY AGREE ____   MILDLY AGREE ____   UNCERTAIN ____   MILDLY DISAGREE ____   STRONGLY DISAGREE ____

ALL RESPONDENTS PLEASE ANSWER THE FOLLOWING QUESTION:

16. My attitude toward the concept question is not likely to change in the near future.

UNCERTAIN   VERY CERTAIN

1___ 2___ 3___ 4___ 5___ 6___ 7___ 8___ 9___ 10___ 11___

ONE MORE WORD

Chapter 6 illustrates a few unique applications of tested techniques and designs which are applicable to questionnaire construction. An important aspect of any innovation is to accomplish that which is intended in the most efficient and credible manner. That same criterion applies to instrument design.

Quite obviously, not every design has been presented. The selected models and designs are included because they are manageable and easily adaptable. The novelty of any design is not in the novelty, per se, but in its utility to elicit more precise information from the respondents.

your designs should reflect a carefully calculated methodology meeting the already established purpose. There are no short-cuts to design. Design is terribly important, for it predictates the ultimate and logical test of your conclusions.

And, speaking of conclusions, Chapter 7 addresses that concept as one of the final tasks comprising analysis of data.

CHAPTER 7

Analyzing the Data

DESCRIPTIVE TECHNIQUES

Designing a survey also requires that you specify plans for tabulating and analyzing the returned data. Since a major goal of survey research is to identify trends from the selected sample, it is imperative that data be categorized for interpretation. The organization and interpretation of data are critical tasks. To these elements, let us now direct our attention.

Respondent Counting

The preliminary step in analyzing data is usually counting the responses for every item, or respondent counting. Either of two methods are used: hand tabulations or electronic data processing. When working with nominal, interval, checklist, and some types of ordinal data, respondent counting is a logical and arithmetical procedure. For review, consider the following questionnaire item.

1. Do you plan to attend graduate school immediately after you complete your Bachelor's Degree?

    _____ (1) Definitely yes
    _____ (2) Probably yes
    _____ (3) Undecided
    _____ (4) Probably not
    _____ (5) Definitely not

Respondent counting for question number one above involves counting the items for all who marked "Definitely yes," "Probably yes," "Undecided," "Probably not," and "Definitely not." Those who did not respond to the question are counted under a category entitled "No response."

A word of caution about the latter group--nonrespondents. You will probably observe that some people, though they do return the questionnaire, simply do not complete every item or every section of your instrument. In some surveys this may account for a substantial number of items. Therefore, for the total tabulation of each item to equal the number of returned instruments it is essential to show the number and percentage of those who did not respond. And, no inferences or speculations are allowed as to why they did not! A nonresponse is not a "No opinion." It is a no response! You only report that "x" number and "x" percent of the surveyed group did not respond to item "a." Nonresponses are often caused by ambiguous, poorly worded, or confusing questions. If more sampling is planned, it behooves the investigator to analyze or seek external critiques of the "nonresponse" items, so that they may be rectified for future surveys. The latter follow-up should include those who did not complete the item.

At least one study has been reported about those who frequently check "No opinion." Joe D. Francis and Lawrence Busch wanted to determine if those respondents who frequently checked "Undecided" or "No opinion" in a continuum were simply a random group within a sample. Their study led them to conclude that persons who return questionnaires with many "no opinions" and the like, exhibit nonrandom characteristics. They found that more nonresponses per item were generated from females, nonwhites, persons with lower incomes, and persons with lower educational levels. They also found that the more noninvolved respondents were, the higher the probability of a nonresponse item. The findings of Francis and Busch tend to amplify the discussion about characteristics of those who do not return the instruments, i.e., nonrespondents, per se.

As you plan for the types of displays of data and tables, you also plan for the merging and separating of data to determine similarities or differences between groups on selected variables. Researchers are interested in determining relationships between the response categories of two or more questionnaire items, for example, the number of males and females in each age category and their respective profiles. Data can be specifically displayed to indicate the frequency of response for each subcategory. Table 7-1 shows one display which illustrates the relationship between two questionnaire items: age and sex of respondents.

Table 7-1. Relationship of Age and Sex of Respondents

Age	Sex of Respondents		Totals
	Male	Female	
No response	5	5	10
19 and under	10	10	20
20-29	10	20	30
30-39	20	20	40
40-49	15	40	55
50 and over	5	40	45
Totals	65	135	200

In computer terminology, the display of data along two or more dimensions is frequently referred to as "cross tabs." Below is a short listing of the more frequent cross tabs or relationships that are analyzed from survey data:

*Age--Sex

*Sex--Years of Schooling Completed

*Sex--Occupational Status

*Sex--Income

*Occupational Status--Income

*Income--Years of Schooling Completed

*Age Group--Response to Specific Items of the Survey

*Sex--Response to Specific Items of the Survey

*Geographic Location of Respondents--Selected Attitudes

*Age--Selected Attitudes

*Sex--Selected Attitudes

Any Defined Group--Any Defined Set of Responses

Typically, displays provide both the number of respondents and the percentage of responses for each cell in the array of information. As the researcher, through preplanning, you determine the kinds of relationships or correlations that are needed and computed. The methods by which you organize the data will ultimately aid in identifying trends, likenesses, and disimilarities which might otherwise not be observed if the data were simply tabulated for the entire group by grand totals.

In contrast, analyzing ranked data necessitates counting the number of respondents who selected each category as a first preference, a second preference, and so forth. For example, the following questionnaire item elicits ranked data.

    2.   Rank each educational topic according to your interest. Use number 1 for that which interests you most, to number 4, for that which interests you least. Use each rank once only.

            _____ Administration

            _____ Curriculum

            _____ Evaluation

            _____ Guidance

In each category above, respondent counting involves tabulating the number who selected a category as first preference, second preference, third preference, and fourth preference. A ratio for each would be computed for comparative purposes. The technique will be amplified later in this chapter.

<u>Percentages</u>. Respondent counting provides a summary of the tabulated frequency for which each category is marked. Frequency data can be converted to percentages indicating the number of respondents who marked a particular category in relationship to the total number of respondents. Percentages are usually calculated for nominal, some ordinal, interval, and checklist items. Table 7-2, for example, shows a method of displaying data concerning the distribution and return of a questionnaire.

Caution should be noted here. The final column cannot be averaged to obtain 81.5 percent. The total percentage figure must be 155/190 x 100. If you simply average the percentages there will be a great error. This point is illustrated since some researchers mistakenly "average percentages."

Table 7-2. Data Display Concerning Distribution and Return of Questionnaires

Number of Principals by Group	Questionnaire Data		
	Number Sent	Number Returned	Percentage Return
Private high school	19	16	84
First class high schools	10	10	100
Second class high schools	74	58	78
Third class high schools	84	71	82
Totals	190	155	81.5

Table 7-3 displays a simulated set of data to illustrate another precaution. Examine the data and the various responses. When using percentages, precaution must be taken to describe survey respondents so as not to imply that 4.8 percent of all home economics teachers have one teaching preparation per day. Any percentage figure is derived for a sample of respondents who participated in the survey. In this example, the report would correctly read: "That 4.8 percent of the survey respondents reported having one preparation per day in Home Economics."

By reporting percentages alone, the conclusions are usually misleading to the reader. For example, three out of ten respondents yield a 30% return, as does 300 out of 1,000. However, because the total number of respondents is much larger, the latter 30 percent might be far more representative of the group than would be a figure of 30 percent which represents three respondents. Stating sample size is important when using percentages to describe data. The number should always be given with the reported percentages to avoid bias and misleading readers of the report.

Table 7-3. Simulated Number of Different Daily Preparations of Home Economics Teachers

Number of Different Daily Preparations	Private High Schools		First Class High Schools		Second Class High Schools		Third Class High Schools		Totals by Preparations	
	No.	%	No.	%	No.	%	No.	%	No.	%
1			5	50.0	1	1.7	1	1.4	7	4.8
2	2	12.5	4	40.0	20	35.1	10	14.0	36	23.5
3	7	44.0	1	10.0	23	40.3	29	41.4	60	39.2
4	5	31.0			10	17.6	25	36.0	40	26.0
5	2	12.5			3	5.3	5	7.2	10	6.5
Totals	16	100.0	10	100.0	57	100.0	70	100.0	153	100.0

Means. Likert scales and ranked data are frequently summarized by determining the average mean scores as a measure of the central tendency. For example, the question below might be asked of 1,000 students and then tabulated. Observe the mechanisms shown in Tables 7-4, 7-5 and 7-6 which convert raw data to other interpretive forms.

3. The course in "Learning Theory" adequately prepared you for your current teaching position.

    _____ Strongly agree
    _____ Agree
    _____ No opinion
    _____ Disagree
    _____ Strongly disagree

The tabulation would be reflected in Table 7-4 (simulated, of course).

Table 7-4. Tabulation of Question Three (Simulated)

Response Item	Number	Percentage of Total
Strongly agree	650	65
Agree	250	25
No opinion	30	3
Disagree	50	5
Strongly disagree	10	1
No response	10	1
Totals	1,000	100

To convert the number who responded to a standardized mean or consistent ratio, a consisten numerical code must be provided for each category. One is shown in Table 7-5.

Table 7-5. Code to Convert Scaled Items to Means

Scale Item	Code Weight
Strongly agree	5
Agree	4
No opinion	3
Disagree	2
Strongly disagree	1
No response	0

In the example above, a code of "5" represents "Strongly agree" and "1" represents "Strongly disagree." The next step in determining the mean response is to multiply the code given to each category by the number of respondents who marked that category. Observe Table 7-6 for the model.

Table 7-6. Preliminary Calculations for Mean or Ratio Scores of Likert Items

Code		Multiply	Number of Respondents		Mean
(Strongly agree)	5	x	650	=	3,250
(Agree)	4	x	250	=	1,000
(No opinion)	3	x	30	=	90
(Disagree)	2	x	50	=	100
(Strongly disagree)	1	x	10	=	10
(No response)	0	x	10	=	0
Totals			1,000		4,400
Ratio or Mean		(4,400/1,000)			4.4

The use of computed means or ratios from Likert-type responses is most useful to researchers. If you use the same Likert scale for several questions, which could comprise a subsection of the entire instrument, then by computing the means or ratios for each item a rank ordering or prioritizing can be made. This interpretation of the data might be overlooked if respondent counts were the only tabulating technique to be used. Agreements and disagreements between selected groups and items can easily be observed in this manner. In addition, statistical inferences may also be drawn from the derived data. That topic will be addressed later in this chapter.

One last note: The code weights assigned do not have true interval values, e.g., a response of 5 as compared to 4 does not have the same value as a 3 compared to 2. The code values could be 10-8-6-4-2. However, in comparing Likert items, a consistent code should be used.

The example shown in Table 7-6 illustrates a computed mean score or ratio of 4.4, which when reconverted back to the nominal categories of the Likert scale falls between "Strongly agree" and "Agree," collectively a very positive indicator for the group as an entity. One could then subdivide the group into subgroups to determine differences, if any.

The methods illustrated in Tables 7-4, 7-5, and 7-6 are commonly used to determine the central tendency (arithmetic mean) for groups. The computation of this statistic is useful when interpretations are attached to data--by the researcher. However, a few extremely high or low scores can make the mean not as typical of the central tendency as the median.

Some ranked items are also commonly analyzed by means, as in the following illustration. Assume that 100 educators were asked to respond to item four below.

4. Rank each educational topic according to your interest, with number 1 being that which interests you most, to number 4, that which interests you least. Use each ranking number only once.

    _____ Administration
    _____ Curriculum
    _____ Evaluation
    _____ Guidance

(Note: To avoid possible placement bias, these subjects are arranged alphabetically.)

Table 7-7 presents the hypothetical results of the survey.

Table 7-7. Tabulation of Ranked Items (Simulated)

Ranked Preference	Number of Respective Responses Per Area			
	Administration	Curriculum	Evaluation	Guidance
First	10	20	30	30
Second	30	40	30	10
Third	10	10	30	40
Fourth	50	30	10	20
Totals	100	100	100	100

To compute the average preference for each category a separate mean score must be calculated. For example, a "weight" of 4 is assigned to each first place preference, 3 to each second, 2 to each third, and 1 to each fourth. Table 7-8 illustrates this method for Administration only.

Table 7-8. Calculation of Mean Preference for Administration (Simulated)

Preference	Weight	Number of Responses	Mean Product
First	4	10	40
Second	3	30	90
Third	2	10	20
Fourth	1	50	50
Totals		100	200

The product of all weightings is 200. By dividing the product by the number of respondents (100), the mean (200/100) is 2.0 for Administration This is the assigned weight for third place preferences.

Using the same formula above, the calculated mean preferences for each topic follow:

        Administration   2.0

        Curriculum   2.5

        Evaluation   2.8

        Guidance   2.5

One could conclude that based on a mean preference, Evaluation is the average first preference choice. But, note that Curriculum and Guidance each received an identical mean ranking of 2.5. Thus, other criteria might be used to determine the second and third preferences. Subjectivity often enters into the evaluation of even objectively derived data.

INFERENTIAL STATISTICAL TESTS

For the most part, the reporting of percentages and means are adequate analytical methods. Yet, if an investigator were to determine whether differences between groups might be due to chance, then either <u>parametric</u> or <u>nonparametric</u> tests must be employed. For example, if a certain question or variable were answered by male and female respondents in different proportions, a statistical test should be carried out to determine if a statistically significant difference exists between response patterns.

In survey research, nonparametric methods are usually used. This condition is emphasized because one assumption which must be met for parametric tests is that <u>the sample is drawn from a normally distributed population</u>. In most educational surveys this basic assumption cannot be met. The use of powerful parametric statistics such as $\underline{t}$ and $\underline{F}$ tests or analysis of variance, is usually inappropriate, although often used. The second assumption needed for parametric statistics is homogeneity of variance. If a number of means are computed for a number of differently drawn samples, the means will surely differ but the variance of the means should be similar. If the variance of means is different then the assumption of homogeneity cannot be met. Again, in selecting samples for surveys, there are frequently wide differences in the variance.

Continuity and equal intervals of measure comprise the third basic assumption to validate use of parametric methods. The measures to be analyzed are continuous, having equal intervals. The counting numbers, 1, 2, 3, . . . meet the third assumption. Most scales, questions, items, or rank ordered data used in questionnaires <u>do not</u> meet the third assumption.

The statistical methods that can be employed when any of the above assumptions cannot be met are called <u>nonparametric</u> tests. These include:

1. The Sign Test
2. Binomial Test
3. Chi Square
4. Rank Order Coefficient of Correlation
5. Nonparametric Analysis of Variance

The use of nonparametric tests is appropriate when:

1. The assumption of normality about the population is suspect.
2. The data are expressed in ranks.

A discussion of the above popular nonparametric tests would require a lenghty and detailed treatment, which is beyond the scope of this book. Detailed information about statistical treatments may be obtained from any statistics textbook.

Use of Two Statistical Tests

Statistical treatments, such as the Chi Square and Spearmen's "rho" (rank order), are used to compare observations and to determine the strength of relationship between response categories of two or more questionnaire items. In many cases, educators will not use any statistical tests. The data will probably be reported in numbers or percentages. Such reporting is adequate where there are overwhelming trends per item. Yet, when groups are being compared, appropriate statistical tests can strengthen the conclusions, or at least determine the probability of a chance finding.

<u>Chi Square</u>. Chi Square (χ^2) treatment in contingency tables is a commonly used nonparametric test for significance. Two basic assumptions

must be met to use the test: (1) There must be a dichotomy or clear division of categories, and (2) There must be a continuum of responses--at least two choices or a Likert-type scale.

In most cases an investigator desires to test if the responses on selected questions are related. By computing the Chi Square in contingency coefficients this determination can be made. Consider the following simulated item. Assume that a survey were conducted among school patrons to determine the feasibility of expanding vocational subjects into a summer session. The questionnaire might contain, among other items:

5. To what extent do you favor offering high school vocational subjects during the summer months for high school aged youth in our school district?

    _____ I strongly favor
    _____ I favor
    _____ I have no opinion
    _____ I oppose
    _____ I strongly oppose

Perhaps the investigator is interested in determining how various aged patrons responded to this general policy question. Perhaps a division at age 45 is made, or age categories which would reflect the general age of patrons who do and who do not have children in high school are listed. The data would be subdivided into all respondents 44 years old and under as one category with the second category being all respondents 45 years of age and over.

Table 7-9 illustrates a model showing these data in a contingency table format. The dichotomy is the two distinct age groups. The continuum is the five-item Likert-type scale. By referring to a statistics textbook the techniques by which to compute the χ^2 would be illustrated.

Table 7-9. Responses in Contingency Table Format

Age Groups	Response Category					Totals
	Strongly Favor	Favor	No Opinion	Oppose	Strongly Oppose	
44 and under	N_1	N_3	N_5	N_7	N_9	N (odd)
45 and over	N_2	N_4	N_6	N_8	N_{10}	N (even)
Totals	N_{1+2}	N_{3+4}	N_{5+6}	N_{7+8}	N_{9+10}	N (all)

*The "N" represents the absolute numbers or tabulated responses for each category.

Using the Chi Square test the investigator could report that:

> The response patterns on the general policy question of offering summer session high school vocational courses had a response pattern statistically different [or not] at the .01 level [or other selected level] between those respondents 44 years of age and under and those 45 years old and over. There tended to be greater positive response by the [specific] group.

Observe how the previous statement is very specific and operationally defined. A reader of that finding would know precisely what was reported. Specificity in reporting results is essential so that there can be no misinterpretation of data. Of course, when you released the information to the public you would rewrite the statement without all the technical jargon.

Rank order coefficient of correlation. The rank order coefficient of correlation or Spearman's "rho" is also commonly computed for survey data when different individuals or groups rank order specific lists. For example, if groups were asked to rank order sets of items, the ranking could be analyzed to determine if they were similar or not. Table 7-10 presents a general model illustrating one use of "rho."

Table 7-10. Model of Rank Ordered Items

Group A		Group B	
Rankings	Variable	Rankings	Variable
1	A	2	A
2	B	3	B
3	C	1	C
4	D	5	D
5	E	6	E
6	F	4	F

By computing "rho" it can be determined if a correlation exists between the rankings of the variables by the two groups.

This technique is helpful when an investigator desires a ranking or preference for a set of items. Although statisticians allow for the ranking of up to 20 items in their formulae, in practice your author has found that the ranking of more than 8 or 10 items is a source of confusion or frustration to a respondent. If several items, e.g., 16, are to be ranked, it is suggested that the items be subdivided into several groups of 6 or 8 so that multiple rankings could take place. This technique eliminates the frustration of ranking long lists. One truly may not care about the 11th, 14th, or 15th placed item.

The use of statistical methods is to determine the probability that chance played in creating the results: Statistics do not prove or verify conclusions. The appropriateness of the statistical treatment is more important than finding "a significant difference at the .0001 level."

BROADER IMPLICATION OF ANALYSIS

In a rather scathing critique, Martin Trow (1967) implied that the nadir of survey research could be observed by examples from the field of education. His antagonism was not entirely focused on the profusion of "one-shot" surveys that abound in educational circles, as much as on the lack of theoretical perspective in most of the published surveys. I agree with the basic criticisms made by Trow. However, there are suggestions for educators, especially those who conduct survey research or are about to.

The leaders of education at the local school district level tend to be pragmatic and problem-oriented. Professors of education tend to share this orientation, except they too are concerned with expanding the profession and tend to be more theoretical. When a school administrator desires a needs survey or opinionnaire in the district, there is precious little concern for the theoretical position that might be explored. To be sure, the representativeness of many school district samples is most suspect, thus the accumulated information from a wide variety of surveys might not provide any genuine contribution to the profession or the literature.

If the above assumptions are valid, and your author treats them to be so, then what can be done to improve the obvious abuses that have been reported? A few selected options are offered for your consideration.

Generate testable hypotheses. Surveys are not done just to obtain information. Often, investigators have predetermined notions of what might be discovered. By reviewing the literature, these notions might be observed in the reports of others. One can synthesize these ideas

into a series of stated and testable hypothetical statements. These
statements could then be shared with other educators who are interested
in similar problems. Collectively, as data are reported, the various
hypotheses could be analyzed to determine which are valid, which can be
discarded, and which ought to be modified for futher testing.

This mechanism can be a collaborative effort between school practitioners,
the university community, and the state office of education. Perhaps,
consortia of states could share survey information and ultimately publish
the more validly supported techniques, results, and hypotheses.

Compare results with other disciplines. Education as a field of
inquiry is highly symbiotic. The basic research is usually done in other
disciplines, such as psychology, sociology, political science, or business
administration. Educational surveys, once completed, ought to be compared
to the published findings of the appropriate disciplines. If this were
accomplished, especially for theses and dissertations where surveys are
commonly used, then meaningful comparisons could be made for theoretical
testing, methodology, and conclusions. Again, this approach would improve
the capacity to generate more valid and more generalizable hypotheses.

Mandate subgroup analyses. The collection and report of a mass of
data provides little in the way of critical analysis. Your author "inherited"
a survey which had previously reported all data en masse, with the conclusions
being overly general in characteristic. But, by subdividing the respondents
into specified groups, and then comparing responses, noticeable differences
appeared. Age and sex subgroups are often adequate for most surveys. As
the investigator, you make the determination on the independent and dependent
variables to be tested. The latter point is critical when one considers

that many surveys could become long range studies having rather important policy implications if the critical variables were explored in depth.

Challenge the sample. In far too many cases, the selected samples are not representative of the universe. Often, educators simply take those whom "we can get." The conclusions from such surveys are usually invalid and tend not to stand the test of time. This criterion requires that those of us involved in directing educational research must become more stringent in sample design and selection. Perhaps this criterion alone would drastically improve the status of educational surveys.

Attendant impact. The test of an applied survey is--what effect did it have on decision-making or policy? There is nothing evil about doing applied or even one-shot surveys--if they have impact on the targeted group. With surveys of greater professional substance, the criterion for impact is--what contributions did the study make to the field? The criterion of impact can be equally but differentially applied to both pragmatic and theoretical studies.

Impact as a criterion is highly subjective. But, the entire concept of evaluation is one of judgment--a subjective quality. If someone critiques a survey as contributing highly to the field, then we should examine the criteria and those characteristics which make it so, and include them in future surveys. Likewise, the irrelevant and inferior should be noted and discarded.

It takes much courage to criticize another's work. But, without criticism, how does any profession improve? Quite obviously, the topic needs further elaboration. Perhaps one of you will . . . survey it.

Let us leave such heady stuff and concentrate on the organizing and reporting of survey data--the bases of the final chapter.

CHAPTER 8

Writing the Research Report

PLANNING THE REPORT

After conducting the survey, tabulating the data, testing hypotheses, and making appropriate conclusions, the next step is preparing a final written report. The preparation of such a report is essential since it is the means by which your results are disseminated. Further, funding agencies require a final report if your research was sponsored.

As briefly outlined below, a report plan includes an introduction and separate sections which present methods, results, and discussion. The four main parts of a report are described below.

1. The <u>Introduction</u> states the goals of the study and describes previous related research.

2. A <u>Methods</u> section describes the respondent population, the survey instrument, and the procedures used to conduct the study.

3. The <u>Results</u> section reports the outcome of the analysis of data.

4. A <u>Discussion</u> section interprets and explains the results, and identifies the limitations and shortcomings of the study.

A research report includes all relevant aspects of the study. At the same time, it is concise. The writer must be organized, to clearly and accurately present the study in a manner that allows the reader to repeat the procedure if so desired.

Writing Style

The writer should strive for objectivity, giving facts rather than personal judgments. Simple words are preferred in the writing of the report. Word selection is an art. To convey the exact meanings and conclusions the writer should strive to select words or concepts that carry the appropriate connotation and denotation. A few rules are listed below to help in writing a respectable survey report.

<u>Do not use trite phrases.</u> "It is a proven fact that . . . ." "Everybody knows that . . . ." If you state a fact, present data to support it. In survey research, absolutely nothing is ever "proven." All results are tentative. The survey, if correctly conducted, simply reflects a relative mood of the respondents. In most cases, terms such as "it seems that . . ." or "it is apparently . . ." are appropriate for survey reports. "Seems" and "apparently" connote a tentativeness about the findings. This is precisely what you desire to connote.

<u>Minimize personal references.</u> Instead of "I believe . . ." write, "the data indicate . . . ." The reason for this style is to demonstrate to the reader that the generalizations and conclusions are based on data collected from an appropriate group.

<u>Be careful of Latinized singular and plural forms.</u> Write <u>these data</u>, <u>not</u> this data. "Data" is plural; "criterion" is singular. You may think that this is being far too particular. No, it is simply showing correct grammatical forms. Your report will be judged on how it is written, as well as what you have found.

<u>Select the precise term.</u> Do not substitute the word "percent" for "probability." Again, careful word choice is essential toward conveying the correct interpretation to the reader. A written report is strictly a

one-way communication device. The reader cannot ask you to reinterpret a statement.

<u>Using "significant difference."</u> Do not write "the data are (or are not) significant." Instead, write, "The statistical analysis indicates that there is a significant difference between . . . ." This example demonstrates how the written statement describes something. In this case the writer must denote that it was through statistical analysis that a significant difference is determined. Further, it is totally inappropriate to state that there is a "significant difference" when using data unless you determine statistical significance through appropriate parametric or nonparametric measures. If you do not carry out such tests, then you must use some other description, such as "The forty percent difference between the two groups in question 18 would indicate a very apparent discrepancy in opinion." Or, it could be written as, "There was a wide range of responses, with a 40-point range being computed between the two groups." Do not write that there were no results, when you mean that there was no significant difference between variables. Here again is demonstrated an often committed error in choosing a set of terms which convey an incorrect summarizing statement.

<u>Format.</u> The format of a report should reflect outline organization with appropriate topics or themes. The sections of this chapter illustrate a sample format. As a matter of style, this entire book has followed a very definite outline format. Have you observed the various headings? These act as organizers which aid the reader. A few tips about format are listed below.

<u>Abbreviations.</u> When using abbreviations there are a few general rules to which nearly all researchers subscribe. Use only standard ones. Write the word and the abbreviation together the first time the term

appears in the report. In the remainder of the report just use the abbreviation. Actually, a monogram is used. To illustrate this point consider the following: "After computing the grade point average (GPA) for the junior class, the GPA was computed for all seniors." It is most important to always write out a word or set of words before abbreviating. This technique helps to keep the reader fully informed--not confused by unknown monograms, acronyms, or abbreviations. Quotation marks should be used to abbreviate statistical tests, such as Spearman "rho." Numbers less than 10 should be spelled out unless written in series, or as dates, scores, or units of measurement.

Tense. To provide a rather uniform style and for consistency, the report should generally be written in one tense. Most reports are written in the past tense since the writer describes an activity which has already taken place.

Write in the simple past tense, except when something is observed in the present. Use the future tense when speculating or addressing issues of the future. An important point to remember is that you are communicating to others. Use the general rules of writing.

Write in the third person. The third person is preferred since it eliminates overuse of "I" or "we." Throughout this guide the writer (Note: third person form) has tended to use third person construction. Other useful terms are: "the researcher" or "the investigator."

Source citation. All citations, quotes, or paraphrases must be identified for the reader. In this manner, the sources may be rechecked or examined by those who become more interested in the study. Avoid using cumbersome footnotes; rather, cite the authors and the dates of relevant publications in the body of the paper and include details and a bibliography. Observe the style of citations used in this text.

Avoiding prejudicial terms. A common error that appears in surveys conducted even by experienced researchers is the selection of words or phrases which subtly prejudice the reader. Did you note the term "even"? Well, it was interjected to make the point. Perhaps the most overused prejudicial term is the word "only." How many reports have you read that stated: "only six percent were opposed to . . ." Used, either with a positive or a negative connotation the term subtly biases the reader.

Inserting the adverb "obviously" tends to connote that the writer's speculation is a fact. Treating either speculations or assumptions as facts is a taboo in scientific writing.

Although mentioned previously, it is commonly observed that writers show percentages alone in the summary statements, rather than both the absolute numbers and the percentages which they represent. Showing a percentage alone is a subtle biasing mechanism.

By reading published surveys, which tend to be duplicated on a yearly basis, you will observe the rather systematic and objective style which surveyors or researchers use. Clear and concise communicators usually resort to using the "Five W's"--who, what, when, where, and why. The first four are objective; the last one is subjective. All are used in survey reports. The conclusions are usually subjective, but based on objective data.

All of the above mechanics of technical writing are the "nuts and bolts." Let us now focus attention on the components of the report.

PARTS OF THE RESEARCH REPORT

Introduction

The introduction provides focus and establishes the context for the entire study. The introduction is analogous to a funnel: wide at the mouth and progressively narrowing to a smaller passageway. The opening statements provide a logical and conceptual outline for the formulation of the remainder of the report. Begin the introduction by briefly summarizing the present state of knowledge. Next, present the process by which the current study evolved. Finally, pare the introduction down to the actual purpose, objectives, hypotheses being tested, and anticipated findings of the present study.

Methods

The methods section provides detailed information about the manner in which the study was conducted. Provide enough information so that the survey could be replicated by a reader. At the same time, be concise, accurate, and precise.

<u>Respondent population</u>. Describe the relevant characteristics of the population from which your sample was selected, e.g., age, sex, education, socioeconomic status, and race. Explain the exact method used to select a sample from the population. Unless it violates protection of the subjects, identify the sample population in an Appendix. Provide evidence that your sample group is, in fact, representative of the universe.

<u>Survey instrument</u>. The questionnaire should be described in detail. Discuss the subscales and identify the questions which compose each subscale.

tate the methods of tabulation and analysis of the data. A copy of the nstrument should always be included in an Appendix.

Procedure. The procedure is a step-by-step description of your ommunications with the respondents, including the cover letter, instructions, nd follow-up procedures. These items should be included in an Appendix. lso included in the section are: how data were treated, how the sample as selected, other details appropriate to the study, and any techniques sed. Precise description of your procedures is essential for future eplication.

Results

The results section includes the quantitative values obtained from our data analyses. Graphs and tables are very helpful in summarizing ata. For example, instead of listing the number of respondents who marked ach category of an item, a frequency distribution table yields the same nformation in a simple, pictorial manner.

Table 8-1. Example of Frequency Distribution Table (Simulated)

Respondents	Yes	No	Maybe	No responses	Totals
Male	15	25	5	10	55
Female	10	20	15	10	55
Totals	25	45	20	20	110

ables can be constructed in many forms, illustrated by the various ontingency tables presented in this manual. Select a layout for its implicity and readability.

Graphs and histograms are also recommended for data display. The bar diagram as shown in Figure 8-1 is frequently used to illustrate data. Not how the responses in Table 8-1 would appear in a histogram.

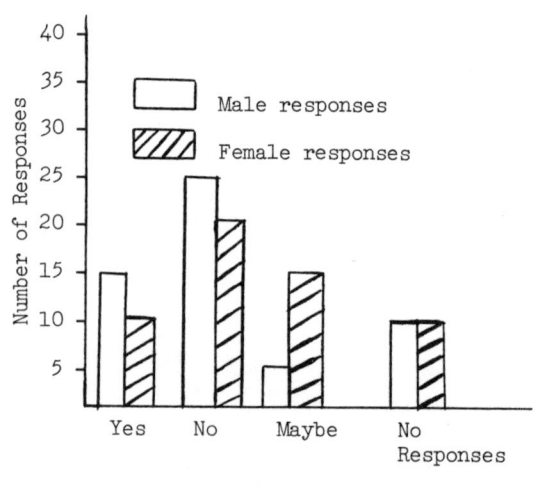

Figure 8-1. Example of Bar Diagram

The bar diagram provides a visual picture of the frequency with which each category was marked, or the total response pattern of a selected question.

The object of graphing is to present data accurately in an easy to understand form. Certain basic considerations are necessary. The axes of the graph are to be precisely labeled. The graph should be numbered as a "figure" and be titled. It must be large enough to show clearly any summary or analysis. The area in which the graph is drawn should either be a square or a nearly rectangular square. Disproportionately tall or wide graphs should be avoided since they convey distorted images of the real situation, and hence constitute a visual bias. Finally, the axes of the graph should not be abridged, expanded, contracted, or distorted in such a way that they give a false impression of what the data indicate.

Discussion

The discussion section, in contrast to the introduction, is developed like an inverted funnel. It begins with the specific conclusions of the study and expands them to illustrate generalizability or applicability of the results. In this section, first interpret and explain the results, then discuss any limitations of the study and conclusions. If appropriate, list the hypotheses being tested. Include a generalized statement of the population. Finally, summarize the present state of knowledge on which the study focuses.

Be extremely careful to identify the (1) assumptions, (2) summaries, (3) generalizations, and (4) conclusions. Each of these four is very different. Assumptions and conclusions are usually subjective in character. They are subject to the personal evaluation of the individual researcher. Summaries simply give a short recapitulation of the survey results. Generalizations are broadly related statements which are synthesized from the summaries.

For example, if a study were conducted by a teacher who found that 80 percent (160) of the senior boys intended to go to college after graduation while 38 percent (80) of the senior girls intended to do so, the investigator might write the following, but very brief, final statement.

> Since the survey was administered without threat, the data from the seniors should be accurate and valid. [The assumption.] The finding here is consistent with other studies reviewed by the investigator. [A summary.] Therefore, it appears that male seniors

show a greater interest in going on to higher education after
high school than do the female seniors at George High School.
It might also be stated that male seniors have identified their
post secondary school plans earlier than have female seniors.
[Generalizations.]

From these findings it seems that more vocational and
educational counseling is needed for the females so that post
secondary school plans may be formulated earlier in their careers.
[Conclusion.]

It has been this writer's experience to observe reports where investigato were confused on all four concepts--and needless to say, the discussions were disasters.

Appendix

You may wish to include an appendix at the end of your report to show all collected raw data, any detailed statistical treatments, or the survey instrument itself. The appendix should include only information that is unnecessary to be integrated in the body of the report. By all means, always include the actual survey instrument.

General

The report should be typed or duplicated in a neat fashion. Use high quality photo reproductions or ink duplicated copy. Ditto is usually unacceptable since it is so often dull and cannot be easily photocopied for further reproduction.

Finally, consider writing a short article for your professional association's journal. In this manner you communicate your results to colleagues who probably share similar interests. Or, if the results are of local interest, then write a report for the school district newsletter. The final report is written to communicate. As the investigator, this is your responsibility.

IN CONCLUSION

This book has been prepared to aid educators in conducting better surveys. My intent has been to provide not just a manual, but a total format. Throughout the book are examples that can be revised with little adaptation to fit almost any possible survey. It was desired to impart one "affective" consequence: that good surveys reflect thoughtful efforts. Good luck in conducting yours!

APPENDIX

MODELS OF QUESTIONNAIRE FORMATS

Within the Appendix are several different questionnaire formats. The first four models are adapted from one survey instrument. The first model (A-1) is the actual instrument which was mailed to obtain opinions and information from the high school vocational agricultural directors in the State of Washington and high school principals. Of 311 instruments mailed, 301 or 97 percent were returned. Following Model A-1, other models are illustrated to show how modifications may be made from a basic format.

Model A-1 was designed to accommodate ease of response; note double spacing, one variable per question, and uncrowded appearance.

Each question is key-coded to an electronic data processing card. Question number one is punched in card column one. To aid the key punch operator, each row number is precoded. If a respondent checked that the major responsibility was a "Vocational Agriculture Teacher," the key punch operator punched row one in column one. All items are coded for column and row designations.

Observe questions 3, 7, 8, 9, and 10. Here we followed the formula of balance. The items reflect all possible responses for the variables.

Questions 5 and 6 illustrate the use of two columns for key punching. The primary reason will be punched in column 5; while the secondary reason will be punched in column 6. The respective row number will be the reponse number for each.

Questions 12 and 16 required numerical information from the respondent. We predicted that the number would be 0 through 9, and alloted one column for the quantification of those responses.

Response categories were precoded by parentheses instruction, ( ) 1.1, where the respondent checked the space within the parentheses.

Questions 1 and 2 are altered in Models A-2, A-3, and A-4 to illustrate other features which may be incorporated into an instrument.

Model A-1. Basic Questionnaire Format

SURVEY OF VOCATIONAL AGRICULTURE
TEACHER SUPPLY AND DEMAND

Sponsored by
The Office of Field Service and Research
College of Education
Washington State University
Pullman, WA 99164

DIRECTIONS

Most items can be answered by placing a check (✓) mark in the blank box ( ). Please respond appropriately where information is requested for other questions.

1. Please indicate your major responsibility by checking only one of the categories below.

   ( ) 1.1 Vocational Agriculture Teacher

   ( ) 1.2 High School Teacher

   ( ) 1.3 Administrator

   ( ) 1.4 Other (please specify) _____

2. How many secondary school students attend your high school (grades 9-12 or 10-12) for 1974-75?

   ( ) 2.1 1,000 or more

   ( ) 2.2 750-999

   ( ) 2.3 500-749

   ( ) 2.4 250-499

   ( ) 2.5 249 or less

IF NO VOCATIONAL AGRICULTURE (Vo-Ag) COURSES ARE BEING TAUGHT IN YOUR HIGH SCHOOL, PLEASE CONTINUE BELOW WITH QUESTION 3.

IF THERE ARE VOCATIONAL AGRICULTURE (Vo-Ag) COURSES NOW BEING TAUGHT IN YOUR HIGH SCHOOL, PLEASE GO DIRECTLY TO QUESTION 7.

3. If there are no Vo-Ag courses or programs in your high school, are there plans for your high school to offer a Vo-Ag course or program?

   ( ) 3.1 Yes

   ( ) 3.2 No

   ( ) 3.2 Do not know

4. If a Vo-Ag course or program is planned for your high school, in which year will it start?

   ( ) 4.1 1975-76 school year

   ( ) 4.2 1976-77 school year

   ( ) 4.3 After 1977 school year

   ( ) 4.4 Do not know

5. & 6. If no Vo-Ag course or program is planned for the immediate future, please rank in order the first and second reasons which best describe why a course or program will not be added. Place a "1" in front of the primary reason. Place a "2" in front of the second most important reason. Please do not rank any other items. Just rank the first and second reasons, only.

   _____ 1 Not enough student interest

   _____ 2 No certified Vo-Ag teachers

   _____ 3 No need for agriculture training in our school

   _____ 4 Lack of facilities

(5)(6)
(1)(2) _____ 5 Lack of money

   _____ 6 Levy failure

   _____ 7 Other subjects considered more important

   _____ 8 Other (please specify) _____

If you are not offering any Vo-Ag courses, you have completed your portion of this questionnaire. Please return this questionnaire in the enclosed envelope. Thank you for your cooperation.

Please check only one response for each question, 7 & 8. Please indicate how you perceive the teaching load of Vo-Ag teachers in relation to all other teachers for each of the following scales.

7. ( ) 7.1 The teaching load in Vo-Ag is heavier than for most teachers in the high school.

   ( ) 7.2 The teaching load in Vo-Ag is about equal to that of most teachers in the high school

   ( ) 7.3 The teaching load in Vo-Ag is lighter than for most teachers in the high school.

8. ( ) 8.1 The "conference or preparation" periods for Vo-Ag teachers are greater than for most teachers in the high school.

   ( ) 8.2 The "conference or preparation" periods for Vo-Ag teachers are about equal to those of most teachers in the high school.

   ( ) 8.3 The "conference or preparation" periods for Vo-Ag teachers are fewer than for most teachers in the high school.

Questions 9 & 10 draw a distinction between classes and courses. Agriculture Science is an example of a course. The number of sections of Agriculture Science which are being taught equals the number of classes.

9. Which of the following best compares this year's (1974-75) Vo-Ag classes to next year's (1975-76) planned Vo-Ag classes?

   ( ) 9.1 Fewer classes will be offered in 1975-76.

   ( ) 9.2 Same for both years.

   ( ) 9.3 More classes will be offered in 1975-76.

10. Which of the following best compares this year's (1974-75) Vo-Ag courses to next year's (1975-76) planned Vo-Ag courses?

    ( ) 10.1 Fewer courses will be offered in 1975-76.

    ( ) 10.2 Same for both years.

    ( ) 10.3 More courses will be offered in 1975-76.

11. Next year's (1975-76) Vo-Ag curriculum will cause which of the following to happen to your staffing pattern?

   ( ) 11.1 No changes in staffing are anticipated.

   ( ) 11.2 More certified Vo-Ag teacher(s) will be needed (expansion assumed).

   ( ) 11.3 Certified Vo-Ag teacher(s) will teach other subjects (reduction assumed).

   ( ) 11.4 Certified Vo-Ag teacher(s) will be transferred to another school (reduction assumed).

   ( ) 11.5 Other (please specify _____)

   _____

12. If you checked 11.2, 11.3, 11.4, or 11.5 in question 11, approximately how many teachers will be involved? <u>Place the number on the appropriate line</u>.

   _____ 12.1 (11.2) More certified Vo-Ag teachers will be needed (expansion assumed).

   _____ 12.2 (11.3) Certified Vo-Ag teacher(s) will teach other subjects (reduction assumed).

   _____ 12.3 (11.4) Certified Vo-Ag teacher(s) will be transferred to another school (reduction assumed).

   _____ 12.4 (11.5) Other (please specify) _____

   _____

Questions 13, 14, and 15 concern some anticipated changes for 1975-76. You will only have to respond to one of the sets. Below is a quick summary.

13. Respond to number 13 if <u>no change</u> in Vo-Ag classes is anticipated.

14. Respond to number 14 if you anticipate <u>increasing</u> the number of Vo-Ag classes.

15. Respond to number 15 if you anticipate <u>decreasing</u> the number of Vo-Ag classes.

13. If no change in the number of Vo-Ag classes, check only one statement that best describes your reason for the Vo-Ag curriculum plans for next year.

   ( ) 13.1 We have the proper balance of classes offered at our school.

   ( ) 13.2 There is not enough student interest to warrant more classes.

   ( ) 13.3 Not enough certified Vo-Ag teachers to enable a class increase.

   ( ) 13.4 Vo-Ag Advisory Committee decision.

   ( ) 13.5 Other (please specify) _____

   _____

14. If increasing the number of Vo-Ag classes, check only one statement that best describes your situation.

   ( ) 14.1 Curriculum officials felt it advisable.

   ( ) 14.2 Student interest was high.

   ( ) 14.3 School patrons felt it advisable.

   ( ) 14.4 Vo-Ag Advisory Committee decision.

   ( ) 14.5 Other (please specify) _____

   _____

15. If decreasing the number of Vo-Ag classes, check only one statement that best describes your situation.

   ( ) 15.1 Curriculum officials felt it advisable.

   ( ) 15.2 Student interest was low.

   ( ) 15.3 School patrons felt it advisable.

   ( ) 15.4 Vo-Ag teacher leaving the school.

   ( ) 15.5 Vo-Ag Advisory Committee decision.

   ( ) 15.6 Other (please specify) _____

   _____

16. If Vo-Ag teachers are leaving your school during 1975 for any of the following reasons, please place the number of those leaving on the appropriate line(s).

Number Leaving		Reason for Leaving
_____	16	Do not know
_____	17	Retiring
_____	18	Moving to administration
_____	19	Moving to Community College
_____	20	Teaching in another state
_____	21	Switching to farming
_____	22	Switching to agri-business
_____	23	Switching to non-agriculture business
_____	24	Switching to non-agriculture teaching
_____	25	Serving in military
_____	26	Deceased
_____	27	Attending graduate studies
_____	28	Other (please specify) _____

Thank you for your cooperation. Please return this instrument in the stamped, self-addressed envelope which is enclosed. If you have any questions concerning this study, kindly contact:

> Dr. Donald C. Orlich
> Professor of Education
> Cleveland Hall
> Washington State University
> Pullman, WA 99164

NOTE: A report of this survey is to be presented at the annual Washington Vocational Agriculture Teachers Association (WVATA) in Spokane, July 21-25, 1975.

For survey use only ID ___ ___ ___
29 30 31

Model A-2 is an adaptation of the original in that the responses use a short blank space and only one number, i.e., the row number preceding each response is preprinted. Parentheses or square brackets could be substituted for the blank spaces without changing the basic format.

The entire questionnaire could be typed in the manner depicted. There is no particular advantage to design A-2 other than its appearance and the fact that the respondent is provided slightly more space in which to check a response.

Although not directly related with the topic of design and format, the model illustrated in A-2 is photoreduced from the original 8½ inch by 11 inch page to one with 77 percent of the area to 6½ by 8¼ inches. Such reduction is easily accomplished by preparing a "camera ready" manuscript in typed form. Most duplicating services now have the equipment to reduce the original copy to any size desired. Photoreduction provides an instrument that psychologically appears to be "shorter" when the respondent initially examines it. Printing and mailing costs are reduced with a photoreduced copy.

Model A-2. Modification of Response System

SURVEY OF VOCATIONAL AGRICULTURE
TEACHER SUPPLY AND DEMAND

Sponsored by
The Office of Field Service and Research
College of Education
Washington State University
Pullman, WA 99164

DIRECTIONS

Most items can be answered by placing a check (✓) in the blank space ____. Please respond appropriately where information is requested for other questions.

1. Please indicate your major responsibility by checking only one of the categories below.

    ____ 1 Vocational Agriculture Teacher

    ____ 2 High School Teacher

    ____ 3 Administrator

    ____ 4 Other (please specify) _____

2. How many secondary school students attend your high school (grades 9-12 or 10-12) for 1974-1975?

    ____ 1 1,000 or more

    ____ 2 750-999

    ____ 3 500-749

    ____ 4 250-499

    ____ 5 249 or less

IF NO VOCATIONAL AGRICULTURE (Vo-Ag) COURSES ARE BEING TAUGHT IN YOUR HIGH SCHOOL, PLEASE CONTINUE BELOW WITH QUESTION 3.

IF THERE ARE VOCATIONAL AGRICULTURE (Vo-Ag) COURSES NOW BEING TAUGHT IN YOUR HIGH SCHOOL, PLEASE GO DIRECTLY TO QUESTION 7.

Model A-3 illustrates the feature of having each respondent code the questionnaire for tabulating or key punching. The respondent places the forced-response code item in a designated area. The placement of the code item helps reduce some work for the researcher. Using this technique, the respondent places the key punch row number in the blank numbered space. The number in parentheses, preceding the space, indicates the question number as well as the EDP card column number. The technique illustrated in Model A-3 reduces the chances of transposition errors by the researcher or key punch operator.

The format shown in Model A-3 requires the respondent to do a little more work and become more involved in the survey. This technique might also be a disadvantage as some respondents might not follow the directions completely and might simply circle the number in front of the response item. If this were to happen, then the researcher would have to transfer the data to the code spaces prior to submitting the instrument to a key punch operator.

Model A-3. Key Punch Modification

SURVEY OF VOCATIONAL AGRICULTURE
TEACHER SUPPLY AND DEMAND

Sponsored by
The Office of Field Service and Research
College of Education
Washington State University
Pullman, WA 99164

DIRECTIONS

MOST ITEMS CAN BE ANSWERED BY INDICATING IN THE COLUMN AT THE RIGHT YOUR APPROPRIATE CODE RESPONSE. PLEASE RESPOND APPROPRIATELY WHERE INFORMATION IS REQUESTED FOR OTHER QUESTIONS.

1. Your major responsibility is:

    1. Vocational Agriculture Teacher   (1) _____

    2. High School Teacher

    3. Administrator

    4. Other (please specify) _____

2. How many secondary school students attend your high school (grades 9-12 or 10-12) for 1974-75?

    1. 1,000 or more   (2) _____

    2. 750-999

    3. 500-749

    4. 250-499

    5. 249 or less

IF NO VOCATIONAL AGRICULTURE (Vo-Ag) COURSES ARE BEING TAUGHT IN YOUR HIGH SCHOOL, PLEASE CONTINUE BELOW WITH QUESTION 3.

IF THERE ARE VOCATIONAL AGRICULTURE (Vo-Ag) COURSES NOW BEING TAUGHT IN YOUR HIGH SCHOOL, PLEASE GO DIRECTLY TO QUESTION 7.

Model A-4 is an adaptation of Model A-3. The respondent simply places a check in the appropriate parentheses. On return the investigator then manually places the coding information in the far right-hand column. This allows the investigator to make all decisions on the responses. The key punch operator would follow the information recorded in the two right-hand coding columns by transferring the column and row data to the respective spaces on the data card.

The format illustrated in Model A-4 has the advantage of providing the investigator with an opportunity to examine each question for completeness. By having the investigator or a designate transfer the codes, the chance of respondent error is reduced, for example, when compared to Model A-3.

Another adaptation of Models A-3 and A-4 is easily made by preparing response sheets similar to the right-hand columns of either model. The response sheets with all respondent items appropriately coded would then be forwarded to the data processing service for key punching, while the instruments could be filed with the investigator.

Model A-4. Adaptation of Coding System

SURVEY OF VOCATIONAL AGRICULTURE
TEACHER SUPPLY AND DEMAND

Sponsored by
The Office of Field Service and Research
College of Education
Washington State University
Pullman, WA 99164

DIRECTIONS

PLEASE DO NOT MARK IN THIS AREA

Column	Row

Most items can be answered by placing a check (✓). Please respond appropriately where information is requested for other questions.

1. Please indicate your major responsibility by checking only one of the categories below. — 1

 ( ) Vocational Agriculture Teacher

 ( ) High School Teacher

 ( ) Administrator

 ( ) Other (please specify) _____

2. How many secondary school students attend your high school (grades 9-12 or 10-12) for 1974-75? — 2

 ( ) 1,000 or more

 ( ) 750-999

 ( ) 500-749

 ( ) 250-499

 ( ) 249 or less

IF NO VOCATIONAL AGRICULTURE (Vo-Ag) COURSES ARE BEING TAUGHT IN YOUR HIGH SCHOOL, PLEASE CONTINUE BELOW WITH QUESTION 3.

IF THERE ARE VOCATIONAL AGRICULTURE (Vo-Ag) COURSES NOW BEING TAUGHT IN YOUR HIGH SCHOOL, PLEASE GO DIRECTLY TO QUESTION 7.

One of the many survey instruments used by the American Council on Education (ACE) is shown in part as Model A-5. The ACE typically conducts surveys on a national or regional scale. The instrument illustrated can be "fed" directly to an optical scanner, which is programmed to "read" the marks made on the instruments. The scanner may be attached to either a card punch device or a computer tape reader where the data are then stored. Note the tremendous amount of information which is contained on each page of the questionnaire.

The ACE uses the data from surveys such as the one shown in Model A-5 to publish extensive reports. As the surveys are designed for long range studies, investigators can continue to observe changes in attitudes, trends, and demographic data. The rate of return on their comprehensive instrument was 49 percent, based on a sample of 108,722 faculty members.

By using the optical scan format most of the possibility for human error which might be made in transferring data to either data cards or magnetic tape is totally eliminated. This system is, however, more costly to prepare and is usually beyond the typical individual's ability to underwrite. For organizations and school districts, this technique might prove to be a prudent choice.

Model A-5 is illustrated with the written permission of the American Council on Education.

Model A-5. Optical Scan Instrument

THE AMERICAN COUNCIL ON EDUCATION

D C ORLICH
DEPT OF EDUCATION
WASHINGTON STATE UNIVERSITY
PULLMAN WASH 99163

NOTE: In the space to the left, please make any corrections in your current institutional address. If you are no longer at the institution to which this is addressed, mark here ⟶ ◯
(Please answer this questionnaire with respect to your current institution.)

DIRECTIONS: Your responses will be read by an optical mark reader. Your careful observance of these few simple rules will be most appreciated.

- Use only black lead pencil (No. 2½ or less).
- Make heavy black marks that fill the circle.
- Erase cleanly any answer you wish to change.
- Make no stray markings of any kind.

EXAMPLE: Will marks made with ball pen or fountain pen be properly read?
Yes .. ◯   No .. ●

(If you want to make any additional comments, please enclose them on a separate sheet of paper.)

What is the principal activity of your current position at this institution?
(Mark one)
Administration .... ◯
Teaching .... ◯
Research .... ◯
Other .... ◯

Are you considered to be a full-time employee of your institution for at least nine months of the current academic year? (Mark one)
Yes, full time .... ◯
No, part time, but more than half time ◯
No, half time .... ◯
No, less than half time ...... ◯

What is your present rank?
(Mark one)
Do not hold rank designation .... ◯
Professor .... ◯
Associate professor .... ◯
Assistant professor .... ◯
Lecturer .... ◯
Instructor .... ◯
Other rank .... ◯

NOTE: If you are now between terms (quarters, semesters, trimesters), or in an interim term, please answer the following four questions with respect to the full term most recently completed.

4. During the present term (quarter, semester, trimester), how many hours per week, on the average, are you actually spending in connection with your staff position in each of the following activities? (Mark one for each activity)

Hours per Week: None, 1-4, 5-8, 9-12, 13-16, 17-20, 21-34, 35-44, 45 or more

Administration .... ◯◯◯◯◯◯◯◯◯
Scheduled teaching (give actual, not credit hours) .... ◯◯◯◯◯◯◯◯◯
Preparing for teaching (including reading student papers and grading) .... ◯◯◯◯◯◯◯◯◯
Advising and counseling students .... ◯◯◯◯◯◯◯◯◯
Research and scholarly writing .... ◯◯◯◯◯◯◯◯◯

5. Have you ever taught at the postsecondary level?
Yes, during the present term. .... ◯
Yes, this academic year, but not this term . ◯ (Skip to question 8a)
Yes, but not this academic year .... ◯ (Skip to question 8a)
No .... ◯ (Skip to question 8b)

6. With how many different classes (including different sections) are you meeting this term? How many different courses (not sections of the same course) are you teaching?

None, One, Two, Three, Four, Five, Six, Seven or more

Classes ...... ◯◯◯◯◯◯◯◯
Courses ..... ◯◯◯◯◯◯◯◯

7. About how many students at each level are enrolled in your courses this term?

None, Under 10, 10-25, 26-49, 50-99, 100-249, 250-399, 400 or more

Introductory undergraduate . ◯◯◯◯◯◯◯◯
Advanced undergraduate . ◯◯◯◯◯◯◯◯
Graduate .... ◯◯◯◯◯◯◯◯

How important is each of the following as: (a) your personal goal or aim in your teaching of undergraduate students, and (b) your institution's goal in undergraduate education?

- Ⓔ Essential
- Ⓥ Very Important
- Ⓢ Somewhat Important
- Ⓝ Not Important, or Irrelevant

(a) My Teaching Goals   (b) Overall Institutional Goals

to master knowledge in a discipline .... ⒺⓋⓈⓃ .... ⒺⓋⓈⓃ
to convey a basic appreciation of the liberal arts .... ⒺⓋⓈⓃ .... ⒺⓋⓈⓃ
to increase the desire and ability to undertake self-directed learning ⒺⓋⓈⓃ .... ⒺⓋⓈⓃ
to develop the ability to think clearly .... ⒺⓋⓈⓃ .... ⒺⓋⓈⓃ
to develop creative capacities .... ⒺⓋⓈⓃ .... ⒺⓋⓈⓃ
to develop the ability to pursue research .... ⒺⓋⓈⓃ .... ⒺⓋⓈⓃ
to prepare students for employment after college .... ⒺⓋⓈⓃ .... ⒺⓋⓈⓃ
to prepare students for graduate or advanced education ...... ⒺⓋⓈⓃ .... ⒺⓋⓈⓃ
to develop moral character .... ⒺⓋⓈⓃ .... ⒺⓋⓈⓃ
to develop religious beliefs or convictions .... ⒺⓋⓈⓃ .... ⒺⓋⓈⓃ
to provide for students' emotional development .... ⒺⓋⓈⓃ .... ⒺⓋⓈⓃ
to achieve deeper levels of students' self-understanding .... ⒺⓋⓈⓃ .... ⒺⓋⓈⓃ
to develop responsible citizens .... ⒺⓋⓈⓃ .... ⒺⓋⓈⓃ
to provide the local community with skilled human resources ... ⒺⓋⓈⓃ .... ⒺⓋⓈⓃ
to provide tools for the critical evaluation of contemporary society ⒺⓋⓈⓃ .... ⒺⓋⓈⓃ
to prepare students for family living .... ⒺⓋⓈⓃ .... ⒺⓋⓈⓃ

9. On the following list, please mark:
- 1. The degrees for which you are currently working, if any.
- 2. All degrees that you have earned.
- 3. All degrees you have earned at this institution.

①②③ Less than Bachelor's (A.A., etc.)
①②③ Bachelor's (B.A., B.S., etc.)
①②③ Master's
①②③ LL.B., J.D.
①②③ M.D. (or equivalent)
①②③ D.D.S. (or equivalent)
①②③ Other first professional beyond Bachelor's (e.g., D.D., D.V.M., D.O., D.M.)
①②③ Doctorate degree without dissertation (e.g., D.A.)
①②③ Ed.D.
①②③ Ph.D.
①②③ Other doctorate (except first professional)
①②③ None

10. In the space provided, write the name and location of the institution where you received your:

a) Bachelor's degree: _____
   (Mark here if no Bachelor's) →○   (Name of Institution)   (City & State, or Country if non-U.S.)

b) Highest degree now held: _____
   (Mark here if none
   beyond Bachelor's) →○   (Name of Institution)   (City & State, or Country if non-U.S.)

11. Where did you complete your high school work? _____
    (State, or Country if non-U.S.)

12. From the following list, mark the most appropriate detailed category for:

    1. Undergraduate major (Mark one — most recent if more than one undergrad. degree and major)
    2. Major of highest graduate degree now held (Mark one — most recent if more than one highest degree and major)
    3. Present principal teaching field (Mark one)
    4. Present primary field of research, scholarship, creativity (Mark one)
    ①②③④⑤ 5. Department of teaching appointment (if joint appointment, mark no more than two)

    (Where your precise field does not appear, mark the most similar category)

NONE . . . . ①②③④⑤	Civil . . . . ①②③④⑤	
Agriculture and/or Forestry . . . ①②③④⑤	Electrical . . . . ①②③④⑤	Industrial Arts . . . . ①②③④⑤
Architecture and/or Design . . . . ①②③④⑤	Mechanical . . . . ①②③④⑤	Journalism . . . . ①②③④⑤
Biological Sciences (General Biology) . . . . ①②③④⑤	Other Engineering Fields . . . . ①②③④⑤	Law . . . . ①②③④⑤
Bacteriology, Molecular Biology, Virology, Microbiology . . . . ①②③④⑤	**Fine Arts** Art . . . . ①②③④⑤	Library Science . . . . ①②③④⑤ Mathematics and/or Statistics . . ①②③④⑤
Biochemistry . . . . ①②③④⑤	Dramatics and Speech . . . . . . ①②③④⑤	Physical & Health Education . . ①②③④⑤
General Botany . . . . ①②③④⑤	Music . . . . ①②③④⑤	**Physical Sciences**
Physiology, Anatomy . . . . ①②③④⑤	Other Fine Arts . . . . ①②③④⑤	Chemistry . . . . ①②③④⑤
General Zoology . . . . ①②③④⑤	Geography . . . . ①②③④⑤	Earth Sciences (incl. Geology) ①②③④⑤
Other Biological Sciences . . . . ①②③④⑤	**Health Sciences**	Physics . . . . ①②③④⑤
Business Administration (General) ①②③④⑤	Dentistry . . . . ①②③④⑤	Other Physical Sciences . . . . ①②③④⑤
Accounting . . . . ①②③④⑤	Medicine or Surgery . . . . . . ①②③④⑤	**Psychology (General)** . . . . . ①②③④⑤
Finance . . . . ①②③④⑤	Nursing . . . . ①②③④⑤	Clinical . . . . ①②③④⑤
Marketing . . . . ①②③④⑤	Pharmacy, Pharmacology . . . . ①②③④⑤	Experimental . . . . ①②③④⑤
Management . . . . ①②③④⑤	Veterinary Medicine . . . . . . ①②③④⑤	Social . . . . ①②③④⑤
Secretarial Studies . . . . ①②③④⑤	Other Health Fields . . . . . . ①②③④⑤	Counseling and Guidance . . . ①②③④⑤
Other Business . . . . ①②③④⑤	Home Economics . . . . ①②③④⑤	Other Fields of Psychology . ①②③④⑤
Computer Sciences . . . . . . ①②③④⑤	**Humanities**	**Social Sciences**
Education . . . . ①②③④⑤	English Language & Literature . ①②③④⑤	Anthropology & Archaeology ①②③④⑤
Elementary and/or Secondary . ①②③④⑤	Foreign Languages & Literature . ①②③④⑤	Economics . . . . ①②③④⑤
Educational Administration . . ①②③④⑤	French . . . . ①②③④⑤	Political Science, Government ①②③④⑤
Educational Psychology and Counseling . . . . ①②③④⑤	German . . . . ①②③④⑤ Spanish . . . . ①②③④⑤	Sociology . . . . ①②③④⑤ Other Social Sciences . . . . . ①②③④⑤
Other Education Fields . . . . . ①②③④⑤	Other Foreign Languages (including Linguistics) . . . ①②③④⑤	Social Work, Social Welfare . ①②③④⑤
Engineering . . . . ①②③④⑤	History . . . . ①②③④⑤	Vocational—Technical (Other) ①②③④⑤
Aeronautical, Astronautical . . . ①②③④⑤	Philosophy . . . . ①②③④⑤	
Chemical . . . . ①②③④⑤	Religion & Theology . . . . . . ①②③④⑤	ALL OTHER FIELDS . . . . . ①②③④⑤
	Other Humanities Fields . . . . ①②③④⑤	

13. In the six sets of circles shown below, please mark the last two digits of the date (year) of the following:

EXAMPLE If Year is 1948:	Year of birth	Year of Bachelor's degree	Year of highest degree now held	Year from which you have had continuous service (including sabbaticals, etc.) in a staff position at your current institution	Year you ob- tained current position or rank	Year te award curre institu
⓪⓪	⓪⓪	⓪⓪	⓪⓪	⓪⓪	⓪⓪	⓪⓪
①①	Mark ①①	Mark ①①	Mark ①①	①①	①①	Mark ①①
②②	this one ②②	this one ②②	this one ②②	②②	②②	this one ②②
③③	blank ③③	blank ③③	blank ③③	③③	③③	blank ③③
●④	circle ④④	circle ④④	circle ④④	④④	④④	circle ④④
⑤⑤	if you ⑤⑤	if you ④④	if you ④④	⑤⑤	⑤⑤	if you ⑤⑤
⑤⑤	were ⑤⑤	do not ⑤⑤	have no ⑤⑤	⑤⑤	⑤⑤	are not ⑤⑤
⑥⑥	born ⑥	hold a ⑥⑥	higher ⑥⑥	⑥⑥	⑥⑥	tenured ⑥⑥
⑦⑦	before ⑦	Bachelor's ⑦⑦	degree ⑦⑦	⑦⑦	⑦⑦	⑦
●	1900 ⑧	degree ⑧	⑧	⑧	⑧	⑧
⑨	↳○⑨	↳○⑨	↳○⑨	⑨	⑨	↳○⑨

14. For each factual item below, please mark either "Yes" or "No": (Y/N)
    - Are you a U.S. citizen?
    - Are you presently married?
    - Do you have an employed spouse?
    - Do you have a spouse working as a professional person in an academic institution?
    - Do you have any dependent children?
    - Have you ever held a student teaching assistantship?
    - Have you ever held a student research assistantship?
    - Do you now hold a teaching or research assistantship at this or any other institution?
    - Were you ever awarded a fellowship or scholarship worth $1,000 per year or more?
    - Do you now hold a postdoctoral appointment?
    - Have you ever held a departmental chairmanship?
    - Have you ever held a major facultywide office such as dean?
    - Are you now a research associate?
    - Have you ever interrupted your professional career more than one year for military or family reasons?
    - Is your present appointment a tenured position?
    - Have you received at least one firm job offer elsewhere in the last two years?
    - Are you a member of the American Association of University Professors?
    - Are you a member of the American Federation of Teachers?
    - Are you a member of a National Education Association affiliate?
    - Have you ever received an award for outstanding teaching?
    - Do you have any student teaching assistants this academic year?
    - Do you have any student research assistants this academic year?
    - Do you actively encourage undergraduates to see you outside your regular office hours?
    - On average, do you engage in social activities with students two hours or more weekly?
    - Is your social life primarily with colleagues at this institution?
    - Have you ever had a sabbatical?
    - Have you engaged in any paid consulting outside of your institution over the past year?
    - Have you engaged in public service professional consulting without pay over the past year?

15. About how many days during the past (1971-72) academic year were you away from campus for professional activities (e.g., for professional meetings, speeches, consulting)?
    (None, One, 2-3, 4-5, 6-10, 11-20, 21-30, 31-40, More than 40)

16. To how many academic or professional journals do you subscribe? (None, 1-2, 3-4, 5-10, 11-20, 21-50, More than 50)

17. How many articles have you published in academic or professional journals? (None, 1-2, 3-4, 5-10, 11-20, 21-50, More than 50)

18. How many published books, manuals, or monographs have you written or edited, alone or in collaboration? (None, 1-2, 3-4, 5-10, More than 10)

19. How many of your professional writings have been published or accepted for publication in the last two years? (None, 1-2, 3-4, 5-10, More than 10)

20. In the past 12 months, have you been engaged in any research, scholarly writing, or creative works? Yes O No O (Skip to question 23)

21. In the past 12 months, did you receive support for your scholarly work and research (either as principal investigator or as a member of a research team) from: (Mark all sources that apply)
    1. As Principal Investigator
    2. Other Capacity
    - Institutional or departmental funds
    - Federal agencies
      - Atomic Energy Commission
      - Dept. of Agriculture
      - Dept. of Commerce
      - Dept. of Defense
      - Dept. of Interior
      - Dept. of Labor
      - Dept. of Transportation
      - Health, Education, and Welfare
        - Food and Drug Adm.
        - Nat'l. Institutes of Health
        - Nat'l. Institute of Mental Health
        - Office of Education
        - Other HEW
      - Nat'l. Aeronautics and Space Adm.
      - Nat'l. Endowment for the Arts and Humanities
      - Nat'l. Science Foundation
      - Office of Economic Opportunity
      - Other Federal agency
    - State or local government agencies
    - Private foundations
    - Private industry
    - Other
    - NONE

22. Would you characterize your recent scholarship, research, or creative writing as: (Yes/No)
    - Pure or basic?
    - Applied?
    - Policy-oriented?
    - Literary or expressive?
    - Other?

    (Note: Please check that your pencil markings are completely darkening the circles. Please do not make √'s or X's.)

23. If you were to seek another position elsewhere, what importance would you attach to each of the following?
    (E) Essential
    (V) Very Important
    (S) Somewhat Important
    (N) Not Important, or Detrimental
    - Higher salary
    - Higher rank
    - Tenure
    - Less pressure to publish
    - More time for research
    - Smaller teaching load
    - More opportunities to teach
    - Less administrative responsibility
    - More administrative responsibility
    - Better students
    - Better colleagues
    - Good job for spouse
    - Better community
    - Better schools for my children
    - Better research facilities
    - Better chance for advancement
    - Better housing

24. (A) Mark all types of work that you have engaged in for a year or more since earning your Bachelor's degree (do not include part-time work while in graduate school).
    (B) Mark the one type of primary work that you had engaged in immediately prior to taking a job at this institution.
    - Teaching in a university
    - Teaching in a four-year college
    - Teaching in a junior/community college
    - Full-time nonteaching research position in a college or university
    - Postdoctoral fellowship or traineeship in a university
    - Full-time college or university administration
    - Teaching or administration in an elementary or secondary school
    - Research and development outside educational institutions
    - Executive or administrative post outside educational institutions
    - Other professional position
    - Student
    - Other

181

25. Please indicate your agreement or disagreement with each of the following statements.

1. Strongly Agree
2. Agree With Reservations
3. Disagree With Reservations
4. Strongly Disagree

Federal aid for undergraduates should be channeled through institutions rather than given directly to students .... ① ② ③ ④
Federal aid for graduate students should be channeled through institutions rather than given directly to students .... ① ② ③ ④
Jobs for new entrants into my discipline are harder to find today than five years ago .... ① ② ③ ④
In my department, it is very difficult to achieve tenure if one does not publish .... ① ② ③ ④
Part-time faculty should be eligible for tenure .... ① ② ③ ④
Teaching effectiveness, not publications, should be the primary basis for faculty promotion . ① ② ③ ④
Faculty promotions should be based in part on formal student evaluations of their teachers . ① ② ③ ④
Collective bargaining by faculty members has no place in a college or university .... ① ② ③ ④
Respect for the academic profession has declined over the past 20 years .... ① ② ③ ④
Undergraduates today study harder than those of four years ago .... ① ② ③ ④
Undergraduates today are more docile than those of four years ago .... ① ② ③ ④
In my field, the male students comprehend the material better than the female students .. ① ② ③ ④
Students should have representation on the governing board of this institution .... ① ② ③ ④
The administration of my department is more democratic than authoritarian .... ① ② ③ ④
A university department's recruitment of its own former graduate students for faculty positions is generally detrimental to the development of a quality educational program . ① ② ③ ④
I prefer to teach small classes .... ① ② ③ ④
Institutional demands for doing research interfere with my effectiveness as a teacher .... ① ② ③ ④
I wish I had a smaller teaching load so I could devote more time to research .... ① ② ③ ④
I consider myself a religious person .... ① ② ③ ④
I consider myself politically conservative .... ① ② ③ ④
Claims of discriminatory practices against women students in higher education have been greatly exaggerated .... ① ② ③ ④
There should be preferential hiring for minority faculty at this institution .... ① ② ③ ④
There should be preferential hiring for women faculty at this institution .... ① ② ③ ④
Institutional antinepotism rules should be abolished .... ① ② ③ ④
If I had a chance to retrace my steps, I would not choose an academic life .... ① ② ③ ④
If I had a chance to retrace my steps, I would choose another discipline .... ① ② ③ ④
Knowledge in my field is expanding so fast that I have fallen seriously behind .... ① ② ③ ④
Compared with most men of my age in my field who have had comparable training, I have been more successful .... ① ② ③ ④
Compared with most women of my age in my field who have had comparable training, I have been more successful .... ① ② ③ ④

26. What is the highest level of formal education reached by your spouse? Your father? Your mother? (Mark one in each column)

	Spouse	Father	Mother
No spouse	○		
8th grade or less		○	○
Some high school		○	○
Completed high school		○	○
Some college		○	○
Graduated from college		○	○
Attended graduate or professional school		○	○
Attained advanced degree		○	○

27. Are you: (Mark all that apply)
White/Caucasian ....
Black/Negro/Afro-American ...
American Indian ....
Oriental ....
Mexican-American/Chicano ...
Puerto Rican-American ......
Other ....

28. Your sex:
Male .... ○   Female ... ○

29. In the four sets of circles shown below, please mark the dollar value, rounded to the nearest $1,000:

EXAMPLE — Your Personal Annual Income (Before Taxes) — TOTAL 1972

Total dollars are $9,200 (round to 09)

Current base institutional salary

Your estimate of the value of institutional fringe benefits (e.g., retirement, insurance)

This is based on:
9–10 mos. ○
11–12 mos. ○

Other professional noninstitutional income (e.g., consulting, royalties, honoraria)

(Note: Amounts above $99,000 should be marked "99.")

Household income (all sources; all family members; before taxes)

30. In the space provided, briefly state what you consider to be your single most outstanding professional accomplishment or achievement: (Please do not mark outside the designated space)

THANK YOU FOR YOUR COOPERATION. Please return the questionnaire in the postage-paid envelope to: American Council on Education, Intran Processing Center, 4555 West 77th Street, Minneapolis, Minn. 55435

Model A-6. EDP Response Punch Card

Model A-6 is really not an instrument model, but is an electronic data processing card which has perforated slots which are designed to correspond to the items on a questionnaire specifically developed to match the card. The respondent is provided with a questionnaire and the data card by the respondent. By using this mechanism for a response sheet, the investigator accomplishes the key punching operations "for free" by virtue of the participating respondents. The respondent returns the data card and keeps the survey instrument. This feature reduces mailing costs.

However, there is one small disadvantage. If the respondent does change a decision after punching the card it is impossible to determine the desired response. One method of alleviating that problem is to provide directions on how to mend the error--by placing a small piece of masking tape over the incorrectly punched item and then punching the desired choice.

These types of response cards are widely used by professional organizations when conducting surveys or elections of officers. The system is very efficient and should be seriously considered by organizations or individuals who plan to conduct surveys with a rather limited set of questions.

Model A-6. EDP Response Punch Card

Model A-7 illustrates the method of printing your instrument on an electronic data card. "Congressman George V. Hansen asks your opinion. . ." is an illustration of another use of Model A-6. However, the model also demonstrates the care and attention to detail which are paramount when using such a system. On first glance, side one seems to ask for general demographic data. By punching the appropriate spaces, questions 1, 2, and 3, were answered. But, when the reverse side was examined, questions 1 and 3 had already been automatically answered as items B and A, respectively!

The printer, designer, and staff person had not observed the so slight adjustments needed to make the instrument "foolproof." Of course, Congressman Hansen immediately cancelled the questionnaire and was rather embarrassed that his staff did not examine with greater care the instrument when it came back from the printer for proofing.

The lesson to be learned from this episode is that prior to the final printing of any instrument, YOU should field test it by actually administering the questionnaire to a small pilot or field test group and to yourself. By following that simple procedure any discrepancies or problems will, with a high probability, be noted and rectified.

To conduct an efficient survey requires that the investigator also be most systematic.

Model A-7. Electronic Data Card Survey Instrument*

CONGRESSMAN GEORGE V. HANSEN ASKS YOUR OPINION

Dear Friend:

The large response to my previous questionnaires has been of great value to me in directing my efforts in your behalf, and I again invite you to give your views on important issues facing us.

Selecting questions and phrasing them objectively to satisfy everyone is difficult, if not impossible. Should you care to make additional comments, please know that they will be welcome.

If you will be kind enough to indicate your opinions, following the instructions below, I shall appreciate it very much. It is not necessary to give your name and address unless you desire an acknowledgment.

Sincerely,

George V. Hansen
2nd. District, Idaho

INSTRUCTIONS

Read question carefully and decide on answer. Push out appropriate box with a sharp pencil. Remove punched tabs from back of card. Place ballot in stamped envelope, mark "Poll" on front, and mail to:

Congressman George V. Hansen
1027 Longworth Bldg.
Washington, D. C. 20515

Not Printed at Government Expense

DO NOT BEND, SPINDLE, OR MUTILATE CARD

1. Sex (a) Male (b) Female .... ☐ ☐
2. Age (a) To 29 (b) 30-44 (c) 45-59 (d) 60 and over .... ☐ ☐ ☐ ☐
3. Education (a) 8th grade or less (b) High School incomplete (c) High School graduate (d) College graduate .... ☐ ☐ ☐ ☐
4. Political affiliation (a) Democrat (b) Republican (c) Independent .... ☐ ☐ ☐

Front Side

PLEASE READ OTHER SIDE FIRST

1. With respect to our policy in Vietnam, do you favor (a) withdrawing our military commitment to South Vietnam, (b) halting bombing in North Vietnam even without assurance that the North Vietnamese will halt their military activity or negotiate, (c) continuing our present course of action, or (d) exerting all necessary military and world political pressures to expedite ending the war? A B C D ☐ ☐ ☐ ☐

2. Do you favor (a) retention of our present selective service system, or would you favor (b) modification of the system, (c) a lottery system, including possible elimination of local draft boards, or (d) creating a career, professional military force through pay raises and other incentives? A B C D ☐ ☐ ☐ ☐

3. Do you favor continuation of the Job Corps and Domestic Peace Corps anti-poverty programs? .... YES NO ☐ ☐

4. Do you favor allowing business and industry a tax incentive to encourage them to hire and train the currently unemployable? .... YES NO ☐ ☐

5. Do you favor the proposal for a federally-guaranteed annual income, regardless of whether the recipient works or not and whether or not he is capable of working? YES NO ☐ ☐

6. Do you favor increasing Social Security benefits, even though it would mean an increase in payroll deductions? .... YES NO ☐ ☐

7. Should the Social Security system be (a) self-sustaining or (b) should it be subsidized with funds from the general treasury? .... A B ☐ ☐

8. Do you favor (a) adjustments of rates and services to make the Post Office Department self-sustaining, or (b) continuing subsidization of postal operations? .. A B ☐ ☐

9. Do you favor a tax of from 2% to 5% on the sale of TV sets to finance nationwide educational television service? .... YES NO ☐ ☐

10. Do you feel that current Federal agricultural programs (a) help or (b) hurt the farmer? .... A B ☐ ☐

Reverse Side

---

*. . . that went astray.

REFERENCES

Marvin Adelson, Marvin Alkin, Charles Carey, and Olaf Helmer. "Planning Education for the Future: Comments on a Pilot Study." American Behavioral Scientist, 1967, Vol. 10, No. 7, pp. 8-27.

Earl R. Babbie. Survey Research Methods. Belmont, Califormia: Wadsworth, 1973.

V. R. Cardozier. Conducting Community Surveys (Bulletin 240), Cooperative Extension Service, University of Maryland, College Park, MD, September, 1971.

Frederick R. Cyphert and Walter L. Gant. "The Delphi Technique: a Tool for Collecting Opinions in Teacher Education." The Journal of Teacher Education, 1970, Vol. 21, No. 3, pp. 417-425.

Marjorie N. Donald. "Implications of Nonresponse for the Interpretation of Mail Questionnaire Data." The Public Opinion Quarterly, Vol. 24, No. 1, 1960, pp. 99-114.

Federal Register. Vol. 40, No. 5, January 8, 1975, p. 1518.

F. L. Filion. "Estimating Bias Due to Nonresponse in Mail Surveys." The Public Opinion Quarterly, Vol. 39, No. 4, 1976, pp. 482-492.

Joe D. Francis and Lawrence Busch. "What We Now Know About 'I Don't Knows.'" The Public Opinion Quarterly, Vol 39, No. 2, 1975, pp. 207-218.

Charles Y. Glock, ed. Survey Research in the Social Sciences. New York: Russell Sage Foundation, 1967.

Carter V. Good and Douglas E. Scates. Methods of Research. New York: Appleton-Century-Crofts, Inc., 1954.

Olaf Helmer and Nicholas Rescher. "On the Epistemology of the Inexact Sciences." Management Science, 1959, Vol. 6, No. 1, pp. 25-52.

Olaf Helmer. Analysis of the Future: The Delphi Method. Santa Monica, California: RAND Corporation, 1967.

Marie Jahoda, Morton Deutsch, and Stuart Cook. Research Methods in Social Relations. New York: Dryden Press, 1951.

Larry L. Leslie. "Are High Response Rates Essential to Valid Surveys?" Social Science Research, Vol. 1, No. 3, 1972, pp. 323-334.

Arnold S. Linsky. "Stimulating Responses To Mailed Questionnaires: A Review." The Public Opinion Quarterly, Vol. 39, No. 1, 1975, pp. 82-101.

Lewis Mandell. "When to Weight: Determining Non-responsive Bias in Survey Data." The Public Opinion Quarterly, Vol. 38, No. 2, 1974, pp. 247-252.

Gail Catherine McClay. "Perceived Role Differentiation and Congruency Among Implementors and Initiators of Educational Innovation." Unpublished Doctoral Dissertation. Pullman: Washington State University, 1976, pp. 124-126.

Frank B. McMahon, Jr. "Psychological Testing--A Smoke Screen Against Logic." Psychology Today, Vol. 2, No. 8, January 1969, pp. 54-60.

Abraham H. Oppenheim. Questionnaire Design and Attitude Measurement. New York: Basic Books, Inc., Publishers, 1966.

Donald C. Orlich, Evelyn M. Craven, and R. D. Rounds. Information System for Teacher Turnover in Public Schools. U.S. Department of Health, Education and Welfare; Office of Education, Bureau of Research, Final Report, Project #7-H-008, 1968, 227 pp.

Donald C. Orlich and Earl Bennet, et al. "Ten District Skills Center Feasibility Studies." Yakima School District No. 7 and Washington State University, Office of Field and Research Services, June, 1974, 110 pp.

Donald C. Orlich and Les Adams, et at. "Tri-Cities Area Skills Center Feasibility Studies." Kennewick School District No. 17 and Washington State University, Office of Field and Research Services, July, 1974, 186 pp.

Donald C. Orlich and Earl Knuteson, et al. "Lower Yakima Valley Skills Center Feasibility Study." Grandview School District No. 116-200 and Washington State University, Office of Field and Research Services, July, 1974, 159 pp.

Donald C. Orlich and Gary A. Rust. "Supply and Demand for Vocational Agriculture Teachers in Washington State, 1975 and 1976." Washington State University, Office of Field and Research Services, August, 1975, 48 pp.

Dale R. Potter, Kathryn M. Sharpe, John C. Hendee and Roger N. Clark. Questionnaires for Research: An Annotated Bibliography on Design, Construction, and Use. USDA Forest Service Research Paper PNW-140. Portland, Oregon: Pacific Northwest Forest and Range Experiment Station, 1972.

Alfred F. Rasp. "Delphi: A Strategy for Decision Implementation." Educational Planning, Vol. 1, No. 2, October, 1974, pp. 42-47.

Gilbert Sax. Empirical Foundations of Educational Research. Englewood Cliffs, N.J.: Prentice-Hall, Inc., 1968.

Ralph Paul Stredwick. "A Survey and Evaluation of Direct Participation of Academic Departmental Personnel in Selected Laboratory School Instructional Programs." Unpublished Doctoral Dissertation. Pullman: Washington State University, 1972, pp. 64-68.

Martin Trow. "Education and Survey Research." In: Charles Y. Glock, ed., Survey Research in the Social Sciences. New York: The Russell Sage Foundation, 1967, pp. 315-375.

Bruce W. Tuckman. Conducting Educational Research. New York: Harcourt, Brace, Jovanovich, Inc., 1972.

Allan F. Williams and Henry Wechsler. "The Mail Survey: Methods to Minimize Bias Owing to Incomplete Response." Sociology and Social Research, Vol. 54, No. 4, 1970, pp. 533-535.

Abbreviations, 155-156
Administrator needs
  survey (see Needs Surveys)
Ambiguous items (see Item
  construction; Questions,
  wording of; Semantics of
  construction)
Average (see Mean)

Bias, avoiding, 37-38, 59-61, 157
Budget, 16-18, Electronic data
  processing, 16

Cardsorter (see Electronic data
  processing)
Categories (see Forced-response
  categories
Checklist items, 44-45, 70-73
  (see also Percentages)
Chi Square (see Statistical tests)
Coding
  checklist, 70-73
  forced-response, 62-63
  interval items, 63-64
  Likert scales, 64-69, 72, 140-1
  nominal items, 62-63
  open-ended items, 69-70
  ordinal items, 63-64
  subscales, 140-144.
  (see also Electronic data
     processing, precoding for)
Communication, written, 91-94
Computer (see Electronic data
  processing)
Costs (see Budget)
Couplet design, 126-127
  adapted model, 128-130
Cover letter, 93 (sample)
  (see also Inclusionary language

Dates, 63
Delphi technique, 108-116
  advantages, 112
  disadvantages, 112-115
  method, 109-111
  model, 113

Electronic data processing (EDP), 73-74
  advantages of, 82-83
  cardsorter, 81-82
  coding, 74-76, 78-80
  computer, 73, 82-83
  consultant, 73-74
  data sheet, 80
  key punch, 80
  precoding, 76-78 (see also Questionnaire, model of format)
  sample EDP card, 75
Endorsement, letter of, 5-6, 106

Final report (see Report, parts of)
Follow-up, 92-100 (see also Nonrespondents)
Forced-response categories, 43-45, 59-61
  selecting, 43-45
  weighting, 62-69 (see also Scales)
Form, convenience, 48-49

General questions, 21-24
Groups (see subgrouping)

Hypotheses, testable, 149-150

Identification, IBM Card (see electronic data processing)
  sample EDP card, 75, 184, 186
Impersonal wording, 32-34
Inclusionary language, 103-104
Inferential statistics (see Statistical tests)
Instrument (see Questionnaire)
Interest, 25-26
Interval scales (see Scales, interval)
Interview
  advantages, 8-9
  conducting an, 10-11
  disadvantages, 11
  schedule, 13-15
  telephone, 12-13
  types, 9-10
  (see also Surveys)
Item
  construction, 19-20
  sequencing, 40-41
Items (see Questions)

Key punch (see Electronic data processing, key punch)

Lead questions, 40-41
Letters (see Endorsements)
Likert scales (see Scales, ordinal)
Literature review, 2, 158

Manageability, 36
Means, 140-144
Models
  interview schedule, 13-15
  questionnaires, 164-186

Needs surveys, 26, 119-120
  administrator, 122-123
  in-service, 120-121
  science, 118
  teacher, 117, 124-125
Nominal scales (see Scales, nominal)
No opinions, 133
Nonparametric statistical tests
  (see Statistical tests, nonparametric)
Nonrespondents, bias, 99-100
  (see also Follow-up)
Nonsexist language (see Inclusionary language)

Open-ended questions, 45-47, 69-70
Optical scan, 178-182
Ordinal scales (see Scales, ordinal)

Parametric statistical tests
  (see Statistical tests, parametric)
Percentage,
  reporting, 137-139
Personal Wording, 32-35
PERT Network, 105-107
Photoreduction, 172-173
Planning, 2-3, 105
Positive wording, 39-40
Prejudical terms, 157
Parsimony, 20
Privacy, (see Protection of participants)
Program Evaluation and Review Technique (see PERT Network)
Protection of participants, 100-103

Questionnaire
  advantage, 3-6
  appearance, 95
  disadvantages, 7-8
  models of format, 164-186
Questions
  content of, 26-29
  placement of, 41-42
  wording of, 29-35

Random (see Sampling)
Rank order coefficient of
 correlation (see Statistical
 tests, rank order coefficient
 of correlation, "rho")
Rank order items, 36, 147-148
 coding, 148
 tabulating, 148
 (see also Mean)
Reduction (see Photoreduction)
Respondents' Knowledge, 24-25
Response bias, 37-38
Response categories (see Forced-
 response categories)
 modes, 43
 percentages, 136-139
 response counting, 132-135
 waves, 97-99
Reliability (see Subscales)
Report, parts of
 appendix, 162
 discussion, 161-162
 dissemination, 162
 format, 155
 graphs and tables, 159-160
 introduction, 158

methods, 158-159
planning, 153
results, 159-160
tense, 156
writing style, 154-157
 (see also Inclusionary language)
Respondent counting (see Response
 counting
Reverse questions (see Subscales

Sampling, 84-85
 disproportional, 89-91, 98
 random, 85-86
 size, 88-89
 stratified, 86-87
 systematic, 88
Scales
 interval, 56-57
 (see also Percentages)
 Likert, 52-56, 64-69, 72
 nominal, 49-50 (see also Percentages)
 ordinal, 50-51 (see also
  Subscales; Percentages
  Means)
 transforming, 57-59

Semantics of construction, 32-35
Sensitive information, 29-31
  (see also Protection of
  participants
Simplicity, 28-29
Single variable items, 26-28
Specificity, 21-24
Statements of policy, 116-119
Statistical tests
  assumptions, 144-145
  nonparametric, 145-148
  Chi Square, 146-147
  rank order coefficient of
    correlation, ("rho"), 147-148
  parametric, 144
  significance, 148, 155
Status Studies, 2
Stratified samples (see Sampling)
Structured interview, 15
Subgrouping
  analysis, 133-137, 150-151
  groups, 81, 136-137
  data deck, 81-83
Subscales,
  Likert, 65-69

  reverse, 65-68
Survey
  events, 105-107
  focus, 2
  impact, 151
  timing, 4-6
  use, 1-2
  (see also Interview;
    Questionnaire)
Synonyms, 28

Tabulation
  Respondent counting, 132-139
  (see Electronic data processi
Target population, 84
Tense, 156
Training costs, 17
Time limitations (see Survey,
  timing)
Transforming scales (see Scales
  transforming

Unstructured Interview, 15

Variable (see Single variable i

Yes tendency, 38-39, 68